Praise for The

"*Elizabeth Vrato brings us wom— —— ———ageous idea
that the law should have some relationship to justice. Their words
and lives will inspire every reader who shares that hope.*"
—**Gloria Steinem, writer, activist, cofounder** *Ms.* **magazine**

"*Tapping into the deep reservoir of leadership provided by women
throughout America,* The Counselors *shows that all of us gain when
we open doors for women. The power and strength of these accomplished
eighteen women can serve as a model for everyone across the nation.*"
—**Donna E. Shalala, president, University of Miami**

"*A who's who of women that goes beyond the résumé
to touch the heartstrings.*"
—**Eleanor Clift,** *Newsweek* **contributing editor**

"*By sharing their histories, eighteen American heroes underscore
the wondrous future that awaits us if we commit to the full and equal
participation of women within our society. These eighteen
women allow all Americans to hope that our nation will someday
fulfill its dream of being a true meritocracy.*"
—**Robert E. Hirshon, president, American Bar Association**

"*Readers of* The Counselors *will be inspired and encouraged . . .* "
—*The Philadelphia Lawyer*

"*A fascinating read about brave women who took guff from nobody
and overcame unbelievable odds.*"
—*The Deseret News*

"*All have moving stories to tell, and
all offer powerful messages to those they hope to mentor.*"
—*New Jersey Lawyer Magazine*

the COUNSELORS

conversations with 18

courageous women who

have changed the world

ELIZABETH VRATO

RUNNING PRESS
PHILADELPHIA · LONDON

9 8 7 6 5 4 3 2 1
Digit on the right indicates the number of this printing

First paperback edition published in 2003

Library of Congress Cataloging-in-Publication Number 2001098268

ISBN 0-7624-1539-8

Cover design by Whitney Cookman
Interior design by Alicia Freile
Edited by Melissa Wagner
Typography: Adobe Garamond, Trade Gothic, and Trajan

This book may be ordered by mail from the publisher.
Please include $2.50 for postage and handling.
But try your bookstore first!

Running Press Book Publishers
125 South Twenty-second Street
Philadelphia, Pennsylvania 19103-4399

Visit us on the web!
www.runningpress.com

For Gwendolyn

ACKNOWLEDGMENTS

More courageous people, without whom I would have never gotten anywhere—

First and foremost, thanks to Jennifer Worick and Melissa Wagner, my editors at Running Press. Jennifer plucked my proposal out of her mail pile and gave me a call. We met for lunch and went from there. Melissa's work, both as an editor and as a passionate supporter of this project, has been invaluable. Our book designer Alicia Freile, copyeditor Nancy Armstrong, and publicist Jennifer Brunn came on board at a crucial time and threw themselves into making the best product possible. In preparing this paperback edition, I must particularly thank Carlo DeVito and Liz Shiflett. In short, everyone I have worked with at Running Press has been terrific . . .

Special thanks to the American Bar Association Commission on Women in the Profession—especially to former Chair, Karen Mathis; former Director, Ellen Mayer; and to Kim Calcagno—for their guidance and assistance in meeting recipients of its coveted Margaret Brent Award . . .

Thanks to the law firm where I practiced while writing this manuscript, Wolf Block Schorr and Solis-Cohen LLP in Philadelphia—for the flexibility and kindness extended to me so I could travel, research, and write—and especially to Mark Alderman, who, as the firm's cochair, was the face behind the flexibility and kindness . . .

Reneé Riebling must be thanked, because despite being extremely busy, she always helps me with at least as much as I ask . . .

Thanks to an old friend, Michele Patrick, and to a new friend, Kinney Zalesne. Kinney didn't know me, yet helped me anyway; somewhere along the way she became a trusted friend and advisor.

For without belittling the courage with which

men have died, we should not forget those acts of

courage with which men—such as the subjects

of this book—have lived.

—John F. Kennedy
Profiles in Courage

It is not the critic who counts, not the one who
points out how the strong man stumbled or how
the doer of deeds might have done them better.
The credit belongs to the man who is actually in
the arena, whose face is marred with sweat and
dust and blood; who strives valiantly; who errs
and comes short again and again; who knows
the great enthusiasms, the great devotions, and
spends himself in a worthy cause; and who, if he
fails, at least fails while daring greatly, so that
his place shall never be with those cold and
timid souls who know neither victory or defeat.

—Theodore Roosevelt
"The Man in the Arena"
Address delivered at the Sorbonne, April 23, 1910

O you daughters of the West!

O you younger and elder daughters! O you mothers and you wives!

Never must you be divided, in our ranks you move united,

Pioneers! O pioneers!

—Walt Whitman
"Pioneers! O Pioneers!"

TABLE OF CONTENTS

FOREWORD

During the past four decades, America has made real progress on our journey toward equality and justice for all. American women, who just over eighty years ago were prohibited from voting, now serve at the highest levels of government. Women are also breaking through the glass ceiling of corporate management to lead some of our country's most prominent businesses. And once denied the resources and opportunities to play organized sports, American women today are making sports history.

But this progress has not come easily or without cost. The women profiled in this book—all of whom have received the Margaret Brent Women Lawyers of Achievement Award and three of whom I had the honor of appointing—share personal stories of their struggle to overcome barriers and of the women and men whose guidance, wisdom, and encouragement inspired them to persevere. These are stories of triumph as well. Justice Sandra Day O'Connor, whose grandmother was denied the right to vote, now sits on the highest court in our nation; Herma Hill Kay has seen the percentage of female students at Boalt Hall rise from 3 to 52 percent; Jamie Gorelick was sworn in as Deputy U.S. Attorney General to a female U.S. Attorney General by a female Supreme Court Justice when, just two decades before, not one of those positions had ever been held by a woman.

The accomplishments of the women in *The Counselors* are a testament to the power and promise of the American Dream and are sure to resonate deeply with many young women who have the desire and ability to make their own unique contributions to this legacy of progress. Today, more young women than ever are pursuing careers in law, medicine, government, and business and, like their predecessors, they need guidance to advance and excel. Just as the women in this book were empowered by the efforts and example of those who came before them, a new generation will be inspired and encouraged by the spirit and achievements of this remarkable group. *The Counselors* is a tribute not only to those who have successfully navigated the challenges of the professional world, but also to the mentors who helped them along the journey.

I know from my own experience the difference a strong positive role model can make, beginning with my mother, who, like several of the women profiled in this book, got up early, worked late, and still managed to put her children first. In high school, my band director and principal were role models I had the privilege of knowing personally, while from afar I admired President John F. Kennedy. With his optimism, passion for civil rights, and unshakable belief in America's bright promise, he gave me hope for the future and an insight into its possibilities.

Now a grown man with many, but I hope not all, of my life's accomplishments behind me, I continue to draw strength and motivation from both people I have known personally and those I know only from their stories: from Theodore Roosevelt and Martin Luther King, Jr., to my good friends Daisy Bates and Yitzak Rabin.

As someone who has benefited enormously from the example and counsel of role models like these; as the son and grandson of two women who were mentors in their own right; as the husband of an amazing woman who, with mentors of her own, was recently elected Senator from New York; and as the father of a daughter I hope will always be free to make her own way with inspiration from the women around her, I am proud to introduce you to the extraordinary women in *The Counselors: Conversations with 18 Courageous Women Who Have Changed the World.*

—Bill Clinton

THE
COUNSELORS

INTRODUCTION

Mentors, Role Models

I can personally vouch for the difference mentors and role models make.

I literally became a lawyer because of Jerry Shestack. My mother was a part-time secretary at his law firm while completing her college education. She told him she had a daughter who was going to be a lawyer someday (I was sixteen). Jerry said, "Well, get her in here. Let me see this future lawyer."

My mom took me in to visit his office on a school holiday. I remember the feeling of fear, apprehension, and excitement while she introduced me to him. He questioned me about school, told me about his practice, and took me under his wing. I wanted to be just like him.

Jerry is an internationally recognized lawyer who recently served as the President of the American Bar Association. He is a champion of women, minorities, and international human rights. No one in my family was a lawyer when I was growing up. Jerry's encouragement—as well as his patience and guidance—has shaped my life.

I wanted to become a lawyer in the first place because of my high school English teacher, Mrs. Geruson. She was a retired lawyer. I remember her teaching Shakespeare's *Merchant of Venice* with pleas for our class to consider the questions it raised about the nature of justice. She would have stood on her head to get through to us. I remember her coaching me for speech and debate competitions—tracing with her finger on my desk to show me that arguments need foundation and have to flow in logical sequence. I wanted to be just like her.

I think about Jerry and Mrs. Geruson all the time—things they said, what I think they would say, things they did, how I think they would handle something facing me now. If I leave Jerry a voicemail full of questions, he'll call back the same day (usually after eleven at night)—from wherever he is in the world—to respond to my message. Mrs. Geruson passed away a few years ago, leaving me enough advice to live by that it will still take me years to get to it all.

Why Not Women?

When I was a college student at La Salle University in Philadelphia, I was not too concerned about issues related to my gender. When I graduated from New York University School of Law a few years later, this was still the case.

Yet once I was in the work world for just a short time, my experiences and those of my friends made issues extremely important to me that had been of no concern while I was in school: the gap between women and men in earnings, power, and positions of responsibility; sexual harassment; discrimination; the failure of male-dominated professions and male-dominated institutions to welcome women into their fold.

For the first time, I found myself thinking regularly, "Where are the women?" and "Why not women?" I began to wonder more and more: Why can't there be seven women and two men on the Supreme Court? Why can't Congress be ninety percent women and ten percent men? What if the president were a woman? What if the *Forbes* and *Fortune* lists of wealthy people listed as many wealthy women as wealthy men? And if just some of these things were true, how would this country be different? How would its agenda be different?

I found peace from the demons that were plaguing me when I decided that instead of dwelling on the negatives and becoming disheartened (because for a time I *did* dwell on negatives and *was* disheartened), I would learn about women who overcame obstacles and what their stories teach.

My intention here is to introduce role models who can motivate and teach others, on the plain premise that everybody can use a little help. It doesn't matter who you are, who your family is, how much education, intelligence, or money you have. If you want to pursue a career, you will benefit from the knowledge of those who have gone before you.

The signposts left by other women on their journeys can show you what has been overcome and how far women have progressed—and make it easier for you to start leaving trails for other women to follow. For instance, in England in the 1600s—not so long ago in the timeline of history—if William Shakespeare had a sister named Judith, who was just as gifted and adventurous as he, what would have happened to her? British writer Virginia Woolf contemplated this hypothetical in *A Room of One's Own* (New York: Harcourt Brace, 1989, p. 47). Judith, she concluded, would have been kept at home while William went to school. And Judith's parents would have arranged a marriage for her with the son of a neighbor, while William went to seek his fortune in London and work in the theater.

In Woolf's essay, Judith was forced to scribble pages in a loft and then hide them or set them on fire. Frustrated, she ran away to London. When she stood at the stage door and said she wanted to work in theater, the men who ran the theater laughed in her face. She was tormented by her "poet's heart" that tugged at her without any means of expression. Stifled at every turn, she killed herself, and the world has never seen a sonnet or play of hers.

This is Woolf's rather extreme way of delivering the message that if you were born a female with potential and ambition—and not that long ago—you had no future. I think about "Shakespeare's sister" when a woman of brains and character is unappreciated or hindered.

In 1929, Woolf opined in *A Room of One's Own* that women could not become great writers for "another hundred years' time" because they needed to have a tradition established behind them—as Shakespeare had Marlowe before him, and Marlowe had Chaucer, and Chaucer had those unnamed men who had "tamed the natural savagery of the tongue" (ibid., p. 65). As Woolf goes on to write:

> One could not go to the map and say Columbus discovered America and Columbus was a woman; or take an apple and remark, Newton discovered the laws of gravitation and Newton was a woman; or look into the sky and say aeroplanes are flying overhead and aeroplanes were invented by women. There is no mark on the wall to measure the precise height of women. (ibid., p. 85)

What Woolf had to say about women who aspire to be writers applies equally to women who aspire to succeed in the workplace. In America, women did not customarily work outside the home or pursue professions until a few decades ago. Now, in the early twenty-first century, it seems hard to believe that one hundred years ago, most women were considered the property of their husbands, and women could not vote. Today we are building a new tradition—a tradition of women who pursue careers—made, in part, by the very women in this book.

A New Frontier for American Women

The foreword to this book was written by former President Bill Clinton, whose presidency was uniquely supportive of women's quest to establish a new tradition. He helped to break the glass ceiling for many women as lawyers, as judges, and in government positions. He advanced the opportunities for and status of working women more than any other American president. He appointed the first female U.S. attorney general, Janet Reno. And the first female Secretary of State, Madeleine Albright. Other women who served in the Clinton Cabinet include: Donna Shalala, secretary of Health and Human Services; Alexis Herman, secretary of Labor; Carol Browner, administrator of the Environmental Protection Agency; Aida Alverez, administrator of the Small Business Administration; Charlene Barshefsy, United States trade representative; and Janice La Chance, director of the Office of Personnel Management.

Mr. Clinton appointed more women than any other president. Women made up forty-four percent of Clinton Administration appointees. Thirty percent of the federal judges Clinton nominated are women, including Justice Ruth Bader Ginsburg, the second woman in history to serve on the United States Supreme Court.

President Clinton signed into law the Family & Medical Leave Act (which enables workers to take up to twelve weeks of unpaid leave to care for a new baby or a sick family member), the Violence Against Women Act (which made billions of dollars available to states and national organizations to prevent and prosecute cases of rape, stalking, and domestic violence), and the toughest child support laws in history. His Administration expanded business opportunities for women, including a May 2000 executive order requiring departments and agencies to develop long-term strategies to expand opportunities for women-owned small businesses.

The Clinton Administration increased funding for breast cancer research. He proposed and signed into law legislation requiring insurers to cover at least forty-eight hours of a post-natal hospital stay. He promoted safe reproductive health services for women, including increased funding for quality family planning. He signed the Freedom of Access to Clinic Entrances Act, establishing a safety-zone around women's health clinics. Clinton established the White House Office for Women's Initiatives, to contribute to the development of policy relating to women and families.

Compared to this record, the forty-one previous presidents did precious little to address the needs—and promote the talents—of the female half of the population. Mr. Clinton showed visionary leadership by aiding women in the ground-breaking work of obtaining positions of power and responsibility. Future presidents who now do the same will be viewed as following in his footsteps and fulfilling the promise of the revolutionary quantum leaps his administration took for American working women—as President Kennedy did for civil rights. I cannot thank Mr. Clinton enough for his inspiring foreword here.

Meeting New Mentors

To further the new tradition that Mr. Clinton and so many women have worked to create, I interviewed a number of women whose advice would be valuable to the next generation and others. Each was a recipient of the American Bar Association's Margaret Brent Women Lawyers of Achievement Award. Margaret Brent is the first woman known to have pursued a profession in the United States. She and her brothers arrived in Maryland in 1638 with a family land grant. With her brothers' permission, she represented the family in court on matters concerning family property, and also made other court appearances. Her name appears over a hundred times in Maryland court records—"Margaret Brent, Gentleman." There is no evidence of another female lawyer in the United States until the suffrage movement in the late nineteenth century.

Senator Hillary Rodham Clinton (D-New York) served as the first chair of the ABA Commission on Women in the Profession, from 1987 to 1992, before she served as first lady. She established the Margaret Brent Award in 1991 to recognize women in the legal field who have achieved excellence, influenced other women to pursue careers, and opened doors previously closed to women.

The Margaret Brent honorees were a terrific interview pool for this book for a number of reasons. First, law is a profession with wide application— private practice, government, business, public policy, academia—and it's one into which women have made wide inroads. We live under a rule of law, as opposed to under the rule of king or queen. You need look no further than the number of television shows that are about lawyers, include characters working as lawyers, have real-life judges solving real-life disputes, or are hosted by lawyers, to see that Americans also love the law as a part of our popular culture. Lawyers make our democracy work for justice—revitalizing and reshaping old institutions to contribute to society's needs today.

But *The Counselors* is mostly about mentoring—not about law, lawyers, or the biographies of Margaret Brent honorees. The women whose conversations are shared here have information and insight that is valuable to all women. Over the course of a year and a half, I traveled 25,000 miles and filled many hours spending time with and writing about these women. I thought, if I can gather their stories, and get them to more people than they could ever possibly meet during the course of their busy days, then I would be doing some good.

The wonderful, generous women you are about to meet were willing to talk with me in their offices, their homes, at restaurants, and hotels—then continued chatting with me by telephone and e-mail. Their authentic desire to lend a hand to others was evident in every exchange.

Through the experience of writing this book I learned that there are numerous ways to be the beneficiary of mentoring: counseling from one-on-one exchanges; observing someone who is good at what she does; or being influenced by someone in the public eye whom you'll never meet. While guidance often comes from those who are older, it can also come from peers or those who are much younger. Stories and examples infuse your decisions with context. This can help in choosing a school or a job, accomplishing your goals, balancing your life, and solving problems.

During the summer of 2001, while we were preparing this manuscript for publication, the ABA Commission on Women in the Profession issued a report concluding, in part, that women's opportunities have been limited by inadequate access to mentors and informal networks of support, by traditional stereotypes, by inflexible workplace structures, by sexual harassment, and by other forms of gender bias in the justice system. (You can view the report at www.abanet.org.) I felt very on-topic and current as we wrapped up our editing. That's not to say that I think all the answers are found in this book. But the topics explored here can help you ask some of the right questions for your own journey.

Before reading further, take a moment to think about who has helped you. Would you have been able to get this far without them? And could you perhaps benefit from more help from others? That's what this book is all about.

I.

LYNN HECHT
SCHAFRAN

It was summer 1998, and I was about to have my first meeting with a recipient of the Margaret Brent award. It was Lynn Hecht Schafran, at the NOW Legal Defense and Education Fund. I didn't know much more than that. But I was eager to learn.

In fact, I couldn't wait to talk to her. I wasn't sure what shape my conversations with the women was going to take. I'm an optimist though, and I hoped to have them culminate in a book. But who knew? Nothing's sure for any of us, and it's no small thing to say that you're going to talk to people in order to make a book when you haven't even talked to the first person yet, and when you've never written a book before. There were variables: What would these women say? How able would I be to take this project from an idea to fruition? It was just hard to say. Fear was creeping in, replacing my excitement. I felt scared.

Lynn and I sat in her office, and we started to talk. She told me she had been a charter member of the American Bar Association's Commission on Women in the Profession. She said that when the Commission began giving out the Margaret Brent award to recognize some of the women who were crashing through the glass ceiling and changing the world, some Commission members and staff were concerned that not enough tickets would be sold to fill the room for the award luncheon. But Lynn told them she was sure the luncheon would be a success, because she believed there was a hunger to see this kind of recognition for women. Sure enough, the room sold out, so the next year the Commission booked a bigger room. And they sold out that room, too. The Brent award luncheon now sells more than a thousand tickets every year and is the single biggest event at the ABA annual meeting.

I could relate to a story about the misgivings that can be associated with a new venture! Perhaps I could even draw strength from the fact that this new endeavor had worked out all right in Lynn's account. I began taking notes, saying, "Well, here's chapter one!"

As we parted, I told Lynn I would keep her apprised of developments. She encouraged me to send her any news and volunteered to look at chapters as I wrote them. Whenever I e-mailed Lynn some text for a look, somehow— despite her hectic schedule—it was always faxed back to me within a few days with her suggestions. With this kind of support, is it any wonder that there came a day when I had enough material for a book?

L ynn Hecht Schafran invites: "Draw a circle in your mind. This repre-sents all the people in the world. Divide the circle in half. Mark one half 'women' and one half 'men.' Within the half marked 'men,' draw a line that marks out one-third of the segment. This one-third is all the white men in the world. Now shade a tiny sliver of this one-third. This sliver is all the educated and privileged white men in the western world. This sliver made our history, our literature, our art, and our law." Lynn uses this consciousness-raising exercise to explain that, "this sliver of men is not making all the rules anymore."

Lynn Hecht Schafran

RESIDENCE: New York, New York
BORN: 1941
PERSONAL: Married (2 children)
PROFESSIONAL: Director, National Judicial Education Program to Promote Equality for Women and Men in the Courts, (a project of NOW Legal Defense and Education Fund in cooperation with the National Association of Women Judges)
1996 Recipient of the Margaret Brent Award

Lynn's mother inherited the world of this "sliver" in the 1930s, when she tried to work outside the home at a radio station. A few days after she began working, Lynn's great uncle came to the sta-tion, pulled her mother outside, and told her to quit because she was taking a job away from a man. Nonetheless, she eventually became an interior designer and had one of the most beautiful showrooms on Madison Avenue.

By struggling to develop her own business and earn income, Lynn's mother was far in advance of her time. Yet Lynn was always conscious that her mother never had the opportunity to fully realize her potential and high intelligence. She lacked family support, community culture, and a peer group—all critical ingredients to career success not given to women during her mother's prime years.

Lynn remembers feeling that those around her had a very clear sense of how boys and girls should behave. Boys, for example, were given cars, and girls were not. Boys were given good allowances, while girls had paltry ones. Boys could get away with escapades girls could not. It was expected that girls would stay in the house and wait to be telephoned by boys who wanted to take them out (aided by their cars and allowances).

Lynn's father, who was a lawyer, was approached repeatedly by politically active friends to become a judge. He always declined, telling his family he had a dim view of the ability and integrity of many of the judges he knew.

These early influences—her belief that her mother did not have enough opportunities, the expectation that males and females had certain roles to follow, and her father's concerns with the quality of judges—helped shape Lynn into the person most responsible for changing the way the American court system treats women.

Training to Change the World

In autumn 1961, as a senior at Smith College, Lynn planned on applying to Harvard Law School until a fellow student told her Harvard only started accepting female law students in the 1950s. "At that moment," she recalls, "I felt unwelcome in the field of law." Instead, she went to Columbia University for graduate work in art history and then held positions as an art curator, lecturer, and critic.

While working at the Museum of Modern Art ("MOMA") in New York City, Lynn first confronted institutional gender bias. "I learned that you were not allowed to be pregnant as an employee of the MOMA. So I hid my pregnancy with baggy clothes, took a two-week vacation to give birth to my son, and came back to work—a pregnant employee no longer! I was so proud of myself for getting around their rule that it did not even occur to me to challenge the rule as unfair to female employees. As a woman at that time, my conditioning was to outsmart the system to get what I needed, not to change the system." Over time, that would change for Lynn.

Lynn's interest in law persisted. Ten years after she first considered attending law school, she started at Columbia Law School with the goal of becoming a civil rights lawyer. One of her teachers there would change her life. Professor Ruth Bader Ginsburg taught her how the civil rights laws that had helped minorities could advance women as well. She credits Justice

Ginsburg with putting her on the path of women and law. Lynn worked for Ginsburg at the American Civil Liberties Union Women's Rights Project; and after graduation, she was a clerk for the same federal judge for whom Ginsburg had clerked after law school.

Educating the Adjudicators

Several years after graduation, Lynn became founding director of a new organization of female lawyers formed to screen proposed nominees for federal judgeships on their demonstrated commitment to equal justice. Her focus on the judiciary and equal justice led NOW Legal Defense and Education Fund to ask Lynn to assist the sociology professor they had engaged to initiate a new project focused on the way courts treat women: the National Judicial Education Program to Promote Equality for Women and Men in the Courts ("NJEP") (in cooperation with the National Association of Women Judges). Lynn became NJEP's second director in late 1981.

Lynn met with tenacious resistance

"I learned that you were not allowed to be pregnant as an employee of MOMA. So I hid my pregnancy with baggy clothes, took a two-week vacation to give birth to my son, and came back to work—a pregnant employee no longer! . . . As a woman at that time, my conditioning was to outsmart the system to get what I needed, not to change the system."

and many barriers when she solicited judges and lawyers to assist in NJEP's mission of eliminating gender bias as an institutional problem in the courts. The principal problems were threefold: First, denial (judges claiming there is no bias in the way women are treated in court); second, the "generational thinking" defense (judges believing that any bias that exists will disappear when the next, more enlightened, generation arrives); and third, the problem of sustaining attention over the long term (courts providing a program on gender bias for their judges once and then believing they don't need to do it again—even though there is constant turnover among judicial and non-judicial court personnel).

She found the "generational thinking" defense particularly objectionable and naïve, because given the dynamic nature of law, openness to change is essential to being an effective lawyer: "When a revised tax code is issued, no one would dream of suggesting that those who were used to the old code—had used it for more than ten years, were comfortable with it—were excused from learning the new tax code, that having the next generation learn it would be enough. . . . The notion that gender bias will automatically disappear when younger women and men become lawyers and judges underestimates the deep-seated and deeply unconscious nature of gender bias, as well as the need to educate both sexes about areas where ignorance about the social and economic realities of women's and men's lives undermines justice. . . . Age is wholly unrelated to knowledge of such critical issues as the counterintuitive fact that being raped by someone you know produces greater and longer-lasting psychological trauma than stranger rape. Judges who don't have that information impose minimal sentences on non-stranger rapists because they do not grasp the profound harm to the victims."

Lynn overcame the resistance she encountered by gathering evidence of bias from the country's courts, in order to make her "case" that there was an immediate need for improvement. "I wanted to make people see women's cases through women's eyes," she remarks. In response to NJEP's judicial education programs which emphasized providing state-specific data to overcome denial, a majority of the state supreme courts and federal judicial circuits created high-level task forces to investigate gender bias in their own court systems and make recommendations to eliminate it. Lynn worked with all these task forces and now works with their implementation committees, making concrete changes in areas ranging from court rules to legislation to codes of conduct for lawyers, judges, and court personnel.

Anecdotes Become Data

The task forces on gender bias in the courts gathered information from trial and appellate judges, court personnel, lawyers, law professors, jurors, sentencing surveys, academic research, and the litigants who use the courts. Interviews with women revealed they often felt ambivalent about turning to the courts because they wondered whether they would be treated fairly or be further victimized.

For instance, in divorce cases, Lynn found a version of the old boys' club. Many judges displayed a protective attitude toward fathers' incomes and lifestyles. Testimony by a father as to his limited ability to pay alimony and child support would be accepted by a judge without question, but a mother would be required to prove all of the expenses related to their children. Courts were unwilling to value a homemaker's non-monetary contribution to the marriage. They also did not recognize that a homemaker who did enter the workplace was unlikely to reach the economic level of her former husband. Studies found women living in economically depressed circumstances after divorce, while their ex-husbands continued to have the same or a higher standard of living.

This lack of knowledge about

"The notion that gender bias will automatically disappear when younger women and men become lawyers and judges underestimates the deep-seated and deeply unconscious nature of gender bias, as well as the need to educate both sexes about areas where ignorance about the social and economic realities of women's and men's lives undermines justice."

women's reality, resulting in unfair trials and unfair results, was also apparent in rape cases. That rape is a crime of violence, the seriousness of "date rape," and the long-term mental and emotional injury of rape were not considered.

Some lines of questioning included gender stereotyping or harassment of the victim. For example, a rape victim might be asked if she enjoyed the sex or if she had been wearing something seductive. Some judges categorized a rape as "non-violent" if the victim was not beaten and bruised, not realizing that rape's most profound injuries are inflicted on the psyche and the soul. To counter these manifestations of gender bias, Lynn developed a model judicial education curriculum titled *Understanding Sexual Violence: The Judicial Response to Stranger and Nonstranger Rape and Sexual Assault,* now being used to educate judges, prosecutors, police, rape crisis counselors, and other anti-violence advocates across the country and internationally.

Female lawyers representing clients in our nation's courts did not fare any better than female litigants and witnesses. Lynn was an original member of the American Bar Association Commission on Women in the Profession that was formed in 1987 and chaired by Hillary Rodham Clinton. The Commission's report stated: "Women [lawyers] report that they are often treated with a presumption of incompetence, to be overcome only by flawless performance, whereas they see men attorneys treated with a presumption of competence overcome only after numerous significant mistakes."[1]

A probable explanation for this problem, Lynn comments, was that most judges were men who had few, if any, female colleagues when they were in law school or in practice, and their wives were probably not professionals working outside the home. These judges had limited contact with this "new breed"; as a result, they were not entirely comfortable with young female lawyers. Judges tended to focus on the "femaleness" of the lawyers before them, without realizing this chipped away at those lawyers' credibility and professionalism in front of a jury. For instance, by addressing a male lawyer as "Mr." or "Counselor," and then calling the female lawyer "young lady," "dear," or "Lynn," a judge sends a clear message to the jury as to whom he perceives to be the more competent professional.

---

[1] American Bar Association Commission on Women in the Profession, Resolution and Report to the House of Delegates, Aug. 1988 at 12.

Breaking Stereotypes

Lynn used the information gathered by the gender bias task forces and the ABA Commission to conduct gender fairness seminars for judges all over the country. Most people were responsive to her; she credits this to judges' sincere interest in being impartial and fair. But she still met with periodic resistance. She remembers: "I gave a seminar where three judges were openly contemptuous. When I went around the room and asked the judges why they had chosen to attend, these three said the topic was so ridiculous they had come to laugh! At a sentencing hearing the next year, a female lawyer asked one of these judges what she could do to convince him that her client was an ideal candidate for an alternative sentence. The judge replied, 'You can start by taking off your clothes.' Later—as part of his apology to avoid being reported to the judicial conduct commission—the judge told the lawyer that he had attended a course about this kind of thing, but had not paid enough attention."

Breaking stereotypes wide open was essential to making progress, Lynn believes, because there is a link between female stereotypes and sex discrimination. Many of the custody decisions where mothers were treated unfairly stemmed from the stereotype that mothers are pure, self-sacrificing, and at home full-time. For instance, a mother

" . . . By addressing a male lawyer as "Mr." or "Counselor," and then calling the female lawyer "young lady," "dear," or "Lynn," a judge sends a clear message to the jury as to who he perceives to be the more competent professional.

with a live-in boyfriend would be treated as a bad influence on her children, but a father with a live-in girlfriend was seen as "starting his new life." She also stressed that distorting application of the law to perpetuate male-female stereotypes can harm men as well. In one case, a judge said he would not award custody to a "house-husband" father because he would be a terrible role model for his son.[2] In several cases, judges showed reluctance to give fathers overnight visits with their infants, assuming that a man does not know how to care for a baby.

Because of Lynn's work, the mood and conduct in courtrooms during the last two decades has changed dramatically. Bias and fairness training is now accepted as a component of every judge's orientation to the bench. In divorce cases, an expert may testify that a woman's at-home work has economic value. And in rape cases, a psychologist can testify that the trauma a victim experienced kept her from reporting her rape to the police immediately after it happened. Judges who think a female lawyer is being treated in a condescending manner by a male lawyer are likely to admonish the male lawyer on the record in open court. These were not accepted practices even twenty years ago.

> *"The concept that 'merit will out' is naïve. . . . There are plenty of qualified and talented women who have not gotten their due because they are women."*

Since starting along her path, Lynn has trained thousands of judges, lawyers, and court personnel on how to provide justice without gender bias. She notes, "Now I'll teach a session about the economic consequences of divorce and a judge will come up to me afterward and say, 'When you explained the difficulty for a homemaker rejoining the workforce, I realized I did not give enough alimony to a woman who came before me last week.'" Judges who attend NJEP's course on rape trials often provide feedback, such as "I didn't know what I didn't know!"

Gender Equity Beyond the Courts

Lynn helped prepare opinion pollsters retained by NOW Legal Defense and Education Fund to conduct focus groups to gauge what is important to our

[2] *Peterson v. Peterson*, No. 86-0642 (Iowa Ct. of Appeals 1986).

country's girls and women. These focus groups revealed that women all over America care about the same things: equal pay for equal work, prevention of domestic violence and rape, and increasing the respect shown to them both in the workplace and at home. Variables such as the age, race, social background, and economic background of the focus group participants did not change the results.

She tells these girls and women, "The concept that 'merit will out' is naïve. . . . There are plenty of qualified and talented women who have not gotten their due because they are women." Female employees from some of the most prestigious firms and companies have contacted her with complaints that their employer has basically said to them, "We don't want you to succeed here."

Even at the "top," women find gender equity to be a scarce commodity. Lynn places a newspaper article on the table as she speaks: "The insidiousness of gender bias was brilliantly 'outed' by senior women faculty at MIT who, in 1999, reported that despite their lofty professional titles, they experience 'discrimination in areas from hiring, awards, promotions, and inclusion on important committees to allocation of valuable resources like laboratory space and research money.'"[3]

She advises younger women to raise their awareness of gender issues because discrimination has become less blatant than it used to be, though it remains just as destructive. Male supervisors may have learned not to say to a female subordinate, "Have sex with me and you'll get a raise," or "Go on a date with me or you're fired." Yet discrimination and harassment against women is still prevalent in more subtle forms—in fact, Lynn believes this form of prejudice is the last publicly acceptable form of discrimination in the sense of the overtness with which it is expressed. For instance, regardless of a judge's or lawyer's personal prejudices, few will say in open court, "What can you expect from a Jewish lawyer?" or "What can you expect from an Asian lawyer?" But if you substitute the word "woman" for the words "Jewish" or "Asian," this is the kind of incident female lawyers still report over and over again.

[3] Carey Goldberg, "M.I.T. Acknowledges Bias Against Female Professors," *The New York Times*, March 23, 1999 at A1.

The huge influx of women into the workplace is slowly chipping away at the traditional workplace model and making it better for women. As a result of this, Lynn points out that women are now less often excluded from formal and informal networks in their companies and communities. Additionally, employers are forced to deal with talented female workers who make important contributions, but who do not have a spouse in the suburbs taking care of their children and running the house. As a result, progressive policies such as parental leave, corporate-sponsored daycare centers, flex-time, and telecommuting—which were championed by women—are being institutionalized, to the benefit of fathers as well as mothers.

> *"Male supervisors may have learned not to say to a female subordinate, "Have sex with me and you'll get a raise," or "Go on a date with me or you're fired." Yet discrimination and harassment against women are still prevalent in more subtle forms . . ."*

On a more personal level, Lynn advises, "If you decide to marry, make sure you marry someone who will be your cheerleader. My husband Larry, who is not a lawyer, is my chief supporter. . . . A few years ago the husband of a judge I know in Pennsylvania told me that whenever he is asked 'What's it like to be married to a feminist?' he smiles thoughtfully, pauses for a few seconds, and replies, 'I don't know. You'll have to ask my wife.' That answer is one Larry could give as well. He is the always-interested first audience and critic for all my speeches . . . the groupie who travels to judicial education programs with me whenever he can . . . and when, as occasionally happens, I wonder if this cause is making progress, stagnating, or even moving backward, he is my major source of encouragement."

Through untiring effort, Lynn Hecht Schafran created a new legal concept called "gender bias in the courts." Judges who exhibit gender bias in the courtroom are now reversed by appellate courts and sanctioned by judicial conduct commissions, and judges sanction lawyers who exhibit this behavior. Thanks to this extraordinary woman, our courts are a fairer place for America's women, and Justice is becoming blindfolded to gender.

II.

PATRICIA

SCHROEDER

In 1991, Anita Hill asked to submit testimony to the Senate Judiciary Committee nomination hearings for Supreme Court Justice Clarence Thomas. She alleged that while working at the Equal Employment Opportunity Commission, Clarence Thomas had sexually harassed her. The committee declined her request to be heard.

The committee later changed its decision and allowed Anita Hill to testify. I was one year out of law school at the time. New to the work world, I was fascinated by the emerging stories of Hill's struggle with office difficulties and dynamics.

Hill's testimony fueled conversation on new topics among friends and coworkers, and it sparked a national dialogue on sexual harassment and gender issues in the workplace. Hill's testimony changed things. After her testimony, the number of sexual harassment complaints increased, and the number of women in Congress doubled in the next election.

How had the committee's initial "no" been turned to a "yes"? Congresswoman Pat Schroeder of Colorado led a group of Democratic congresswomen in approaching Senate Majority Leader George Mitchell (D-Maine) to use his influence to bring Anita Hill before the committee. Nine congresswomen, among them Schroeder, Patsy Mink (D-Hawaii), and Barbara Boxer (D-California), interrupted Mitchell during a Senate luncheon and asked him to meet with them in his office. He did, and with his support Anita Hill testified before the committee.

Without Schroeder's initiative—and willingness to stand up for someone she had never met—Anita Hill probably would not have been heard. Schroeder was accustomed to struggles in politics, however; she was first elected to Congress in 1972, when women were just breaking through the glass ceiling in many professions. She faced struggles large and small, daily and constant, just like millions of other American working women.

It was with great anticipation that I climbed the steps on a busy Washington, D.C., street to Pat Schroeder's office, to learn more about this former congresswoman who has spent so much of her career standing up for herself and for millions of other Americans who've only recently had a voice in politics.

"The White House might as well have a 'No Girls Allowed' sign posted on the door," Pat Schroeder notes. The number of women who have pursued the United States presidency can be counted on one hand. Pat launched her campaign in 1987. Before her were Shirley Chisholm (1972), Belva Lockwood (1884), and Victoria Woodhull (1872), and in 2000 Elizabeth Dole added her name to the list.

Pat has spent her life tearing down "No Girls Allowed" signs. When she began attending Harvard Law School in 1961, there were only fifteen women in her first-year class of more than five hundred. She remembers male students changing their seat assignments in the lecture halls so they would not have to sit next to a female law student. "Infiltrating the boys' club of Harvard prepared me for infiltrating the boys' club of Congress," Pat observes.

After Pat and her husband, James, graduated from Harvard Law School together in 1964, they settled in Denver, Colorado. Pat practiced and taught law for several years. Then she was approached by a local committee searching for a candidate to run against the Republican incumbent in their district. She won that seat and entered the Ninety-third Congress in 1972.

Patricia Schroeder

RESIDENCE: Washington, D.C.
HOMETOWN: Denver, Colorado
BORN: 1940
PERSONAL: Married (two children)
PROFESSIONAL: President of the Association of American Publishers, and formerly a twelve-term U.S. Congresswoman
NUMBER OF POLITICAL CONSULTANTS HIRED AND POLLS TAKEN WHILE SERVING TWENTY-FOUR YEARS IN CONGRESS: Zero
1996 Recipient of the Margaret Brent Award

Sharing a Seat on the Armed Services Committee

Upon her arrival to Congress, Pat faced one of her biggest challenges as a congresswoman—she set out to become the first female member of the prestigious U.S. House of Representatives' Armed Services Committee. The committee was extremely powerful. At that time, it controlled about sixty-five cents of every dollar Congress spent—but no woman had ever breached this sacred male bastion.

Pat's biggest opposition to her appointment was a formidable opponent, the committee's chairman, F. Edward Hebert of Louisiana. He was dead set against women or minorities becoming members of his committee. "When I arrived in Congress, these chairmen were demigods. Younger representatives were expected to be quiet, wait their turn, and hope they could outlive their opposition! Everyone was afraid of Hebert . . . Armed Services was the most powerful committee in Congress during the Vietnam War, and Hebert ran it like a personal fiefdom."

Remarkably, Pat succeeded in her quest for an appointment to the committee. But when she and a fellow representative, Ron Dellums (a Democrat from California and the first African-American to be appointed to the committee) arrived for their first meeting, they found only one open chair in the committee meeting room. Apparently Hebert, furious that his veto of their appointments was ignored, had announced that women and African-Americans were worth only half of one "regular" member, so he allowed only one new chair to be added to the room for his two new "half" members. None of the other forty-two committee members offered to get them another chair—many of them had military bases in their districts, so they felt they had a vested interest "to please the chairman, no matter how outrageous he was!" Pat expounds, "They felt their political careers depended upon their being able to go home and tell their constituents, 'Look how much money I got for you this year for our base.'

"Infiltrating the boys' club of Harvard prepared me for infiltrating the boys' club of Congress."

"Ron and I had two choices over the chair. We could go ballistic or we could hang in there." Pat and Ron decided they did not want to jeopardize their appointment to the most powerful House committee by starting a commotion over the lack of a seat, so they sat together on one chair. "We were 'cheek to cheek,' trying to retain our dignity." Not surprisingly given their close quarters, Pat and Ron became great friends and supporters of each other. "Once, in a heated debate, Ron said to Hebert, 'There are only two of us with the balls to stand up against what we all know is wrong.' I tugged on his arm and suggested 'balls' was not a precisely accurate description of our little coalition of two."

Pat exercised her right as a committee member to attach to the annual defense budget bill her individual views not shared by the committee. She submitted supplemental reports about Pentagon practices. She provided alternative defense budgets, suggesting that NATO allies contribute more money, or pointing out that while some weapon systems worked, others weren't at all reliable. Some colleagues thought her motivation was to goad Hebert, but that was not the case. Pat considered the submission of supplements with alternative views as part of her duty as a free-thinking committee member. She continued to include supplements expressing her views during her entire tenure on the committee, even after Hebert was gone.

Hebert, furious that his veto of their appointments was ignored, had announced that women and African-Americans were worth only half of one "regular" member, so he allowed only one new chair to be added to the room for his two new "half" members.

Repeatedly, she felt committee members were afraid of Hebert and, even more, afraid of vigorous, open debate about the role of the military. When she asserted her views, a frequent refrain from committee members was, "What could she know? She never served in the military." Yet most of them had not served in the military either.

Committee members who criticized Pat were just following the example of their chairman. Hebert continually characterized her efforts in the most denigrating light. "I questioned U.S. bombing raids on Cambodia, and he said, 'I wish you'd support our boys like you support the enemy.' And when I voted to cut off the funds for the continued bombing, he yelled, 'No! That's the dumbest thing I ever heard!'"

Hebert's hold on the Armed Services Committee was finally challenged when the first group of post-Watergate representatives came to Washington in 1974. These representatives had been elected in a wave of voter backlash against the perceived corruption in Washington, D.C. The reform-oriented representatives requested a report from the chairman of each committee on progress and goals. Because of them, chairmanship was changed from an appointed position to an elected one, with a secret ballot every term. "Hebert had been branded as an autocrat, in part because word was getting around about the way he had been treating me and Ron over the past two years. The freshmen decided Hebert should be voted out. He tried to campaign for votes, but it was too late." And with Hebert's replacement, Pat and Ron had chairs of their own. (Ron Dellums would later serve as chair of the committee, from 1992 to 1994.)

Taking a Stand

Pat believes often just the willingness to stand up for yourself—though in her case it was to sit down for herself—and to remain tenacious are the most effective means to an end. She points out that she learned this lesson in part due to a very difficult situation: The second time Pat was pregnant, which was before she entered Congress, she started to bleed in her fourth month. Her obstetrician brushed off her concerns. "He called me high strung, and said that since I was a Harvard lawyer, I must be having trouble adjusting to life as a housewife."

Two months before her due date, she went into labor. In the delivery room, it was discovered that Pat had been carrying twins, a boy and a girl. The girl died early in the pregnancy and had been the cause of the hemorrhaging. The boy was born barely alive, weighing only four and one half pounds, and died by the next morning. Pat explains, "I was angry at the doctor for refusing to listen to me, but I was furious at myself for letting a doctor convince me I had no right to question his judgment." She has never forgotten this lesson brought home in tragedy.

A Pioneering Campaign

Most of the time, Pat has stood up not only for herself, but she has also embraced what some have called "women's issues"—but which she calls "American issues"—involving fairness, equality, and justice. Nowhere was this more evident than in her historic Presidential campaign.

In the spring of 1987, during her tenure as a congresswoman from Denver, Pat cochaired the presidential campaign of Senator Gary Hart of Colorado. The campaign fell on hard times when Hart, who was married, defended himself against accusations of womanizing by daring the press to "go ahead and follow me." Shortly thereafter, the *Miami Herald* obtained photographs of him on a yacht with a woman named Donna Rice on his lap. His campaign dissolved virtually overnight, and Pat's role as cochair came to an abrupt end.

However, Pat's supporters urged her to take a look at joining the presidential race herself. She recollects, "I asked myself, 'Could I raise the necessary money? Build an organization? Be accepted?'" Pat's largest obstacle was time. Seven other Democrats already had been running for some time. Also, there was the issue of her gender—Pat would be the first woman to make an attempt at the presidency since 1972,

"I was angry at the doctor for refusing to listen to me, but I was furious at myself for letting a doctor convince me I had no right to question his judgment."

and though it had been fifteen years since Shirley Chisholm had unsuccessfully given it a go, there were no real indications that mainstream voters were ready to embrace her candidacy.

Pat nonetheless decided to throw her hat in the ring. She knew she could not win, but she also knew she could add something to the candidates' debates that was not being addressed by her male counterparts: a discussion of family issues with the American people. It was an important subject that needed to be addressed, and she felt that she was the person to bring it to the forefront.

"Can you even imagine a male candidate being asked the outrageous question of whether his wife knows if he is running for president?"

As she campaigned, the anticipated focus on her gender began. She found some aspects of it amusing—and some annoying. The press called her "the women's candidate" and measured women's progress in society by her candidacy. At one of her appearances, a state Democratic Party chairman introduced her in glowing terms, then ended with, "Of course I can't vote for her because I have a problem with a man for first lady." At other events, she was asked, "Does your husband know you're running?" Pat queries, "Can you even imagine a male candidate being asked the outrageous question of whether his wife knows if he is running for president?"

As she campaigned, she was struck by how ready people were to talk candidly about family issues. Audiences of mixed gender asked how she managed to be in Congress, have a spouse, and raise two children. Men had been running for president for generations, and they were never asked these types of questions because it was assumed their wives handled all the domestic responsibilities. Pat found that "men and women, from college students to senior citizens, wanted politicians who understand what is going on in their lives and government policies that reflect that understanding. Americans were desperate for someone to help them juggle all the roles and chores modern life has laid upon them."

Out of this dialogue with the American electorate, Pat became convinced that people needed government policies to help them with burgeoning family and health care issues. As the modern age progressed, more and more families needed two incomes to survive financially, but the government had done little to address this change. Pat explains, "After World War II, America was the world's 911 number. We poured money into providing the world's military defense, while our allies put money into paid health care, free college tuition, and excellent childcare for their citizens. They could afford these programs because we denied them to ourselves in order to provide the world's defense." Pat wanted our government to have more policies to help families.

When August arrived, Pat ranked third for the Democratic nomination in a *Time* magazine poll, but she felt that winning would have taken more money and time than she was able to give. Reluctantly, she decided to withdraw from the race. In the end, finances triumphed. "I just didn't have enough money to be truly competitive," she reflects. "All along, people had been saying, 'It would be really interesting if you ran,' and I thought that meant they would support me. Some did, and some just thought, 'How nice—the race is more interesting.' It was a reality check. I wanted to be president, not interesting! Other politicians were hesitant to put their own careers on the line by actively saying I was a viable candidate."

She began to cry while delivering the farewell speech of her campaign— emotions overwhelmed her as she looked into her parents' eyes, as the audience groaned, as people chanted "Run, Pat, run." The political climate is so different now that it is hard to imagine the response Pat received to her tears. She recounts, "Those seventeen seconds were treated like a total breakdown. . . . I went on with my speech, but it was my tears that got the headlines, not my words."

The media discussed her tears for weeks. "Some writers went so far as to say that my tears had dampened all

"Traditionally, politics has not been a field for women to pursue, but we are just as able and have just as much to offer as men."

hopes for women in presidential politics for the rest of this century," she recalls. The critics who angered her the most were "the ones who said they wouldn't want the person who had their finger on the nuclear button to be someone who cries . . . but I wouldn't want that person to be someone who doesn't cry!" In response to all the media attention, Pat started a "sob sister" file. It included news items on the public tears of Ronald Reagan, George Bush Sr., Margaret Thatcher, and Oliver North. After the media commotion her own tears had caused, Pat got some satisfaction in finding that other political figures also cried in public. She points out, "Now crying is something male politicians need to do to show they're compassionate. . . . Crying came out of the closet."

Pat Schroeder not only brought crying out of the closet, she also showed the nation that traditional feminine qualities can be leadership qualities. In the years following Pat's pioneering campaign, issues important to American families have become a priority in politics. Pat sponsored the Family Leave and Medical Act (1993) and the Violence Against Women and Child Abuse Protection Act (1994). She was instrumental in the passage of the Health Care Equity Act, which guarantees adequate funding for women's health issues, and she served as a cochair of the bipartisan Congressional Women's Caucus.

"I'm passing this torch. . . . Come and get it!"

Today, she characterizes her candidacy as a quest for the answer to the question, "Is America 'man' enough to back a woman?" The answer, she found then, was "No!" It is probably still the answer.

Passing the Torch

When she left Congress in 1996 after serving for twenty-four years—making her the longest sitting female member of Congress—Pat taught at Princeton University's graduate school of public service. She was both amazed and dismayed to discover that most of her students had no intention of ever running for public office. Pat wants young women to aspire to serve in Congress. She believes that only when women reach a critical mass in Congress will they make a real difference. "Traditionally, politics has not been a field for women to pursue, but we are just as able and have just as much to offer as men."

Pat also encourages young women to become comfortable with the term "feminist," as it is a term and philosophy designed to help them. Pat says, "I can't tell you how many girls and young women I have met who insist they are not 'feminists.' . . . I don't know how they came to associate feminism only with mythical acts like bra-burning. But I always think, 'Give it a couple years out in the work world, and then we'll talk.' Sure enough, so many working women came into my congressional office to complain about the unfairness of lower pay or some favoritism shown to male counterparts. . . . And I'd say, 'Welcome to feminism!'"

Seated, Pat sets down her glass of ice water, raises her arm in the air, gives her characteristic Cheshire cat smile, and says, "I'm passing this torch. . . . Come and get it!"

It is time for a new group of American women to pull down some of those "No Girls Allowed" signs.

III.
LOUISE
RAGGIO

Growing up in Philadelphia, the cradle of American liberty, I cannot even count how many times I visited my city's historic sights. Suffice it to say that Independence Hall, the Liberty Bell, Betsy Ross' house, and Benjamin Franklin's house were popular field trips in grade school.

I thought Benjamin Franklin was cool. He tried his hand at so many different things. He conducted experiments with a kite and a key in a storm to prove there is electricity in lightning. He was the author and publisher of Poor Richard's Almanack. *He invented bifocals, signed the Declaration of Independence, and served as United States Ambassador to France. He said many quaint but catchy—and substantive—things like, "Little strokes fell oaks" and "Keep thy shop, and thy shop will keep thee."*

During one of the colonial America tours, I learned Franklin used to start each day by asking himself, "What good shall I do this day?" And at the end of the day, he examined his conduct by asking, "What good have I done this day?"

So from time to time, brushing my teeth or getting ready for school, I used to think of Ben Franklin and label something I was going to do that day as "good." Then I grew up, went to college, left Philly, and didn't think about Ben Franklin while brushing my teeth anymore.

The concept of examination of a day, or a life, came to the forefront again when I met Louise Raggio. This time, I was at an age and a point in my life where I could really appreciate it. Louise is a Texan octogenarian who meets the tests life provides head-on. "What a good person," I said to myself repeatedly as I listened to Louise and thought about her afterward.

I tried to put myself in Louise's shoes. What if I were eighty-something years old and telling someone I had never met before about the way I had been spending decades of time? Just what would I have to say for myself?

I thought about the people I hope will be with me and the work I hope will engross me in the decades to come. Now there is another layer over everything I do, and I know it wasn't there even a few years ago. It's the layer of—no matter what I'm doing—being conscious of the question, "How am I living this life of mine, as I go around doing these things that are important to me?"

Thank you for that, Mr. Franklin and Ms. Raggio.

At the age of twenty-two, Louise Raggio thought she had an ideal life ahead of her. Her plan was to marry the lawyer she had fallen in love with and then stay home, be a lawyer's wife, and raise their family. She planned on spending spare time volunteering for church and community affairs. With a twinkle in her eye, she says, "If you want to make God laugh, go ahead and make a lot of plans for yourself!"

Louise Raggio

RESIDENCE: Dallas, Texas
BORN: 1919
PERSONAL: Widowed
(Three sons, all practice law
with her)
PROFESSIONAL: Partner in
the law firm Raggio & Raggio
PLLC
*1995 Recipient of the
Margaret Brent Award*

Louise did do some of what she planned. She married the lawyer. She raised three sons. She was involved in her church and her community. But she never did get to stay home and be a lawyer's wife.

World War II intervened and changed the course of her life. Louise never told close friends and relatives the full story. They saw Louise grow into a feminist lawyer who transformed the face of law for women in Texas. She kept silent in order to protect her husband, and even now she is willing to tell the whole story only because he has passed away. The story involves a slice of World War II history. It tells her answer to the question "What makes a feminist?" and contains lessons in loyalty and strong character.

Finest Hours

Louise met her husband, Grier, when they were both working for government agencies in Austin, Texas. On their very first date, he told her they would marry. She remembers, "I just thought he was being a smoothie—he was tall, handsome, personable." But Louise found herself falling for the smoothie lawyer, and Grier's assessment of their compatibility was accurate. In April 1941, after knowing each other just three months, they married.

On December 7, 1941, the Japanese bombed the U.S. naval base at Pearl Harbor, Hawaii, and the United States entered World War II against Japan and Germany. Louise had found out she was pregnant just days before. Grier obtained permission to delay going overseas until their baby was born. When Louise gave birth to Grier Jr., Grier left for the South Pacific. The husband who left Louise to go to war was not the same man who came back.

As part of his military service, Grier was sent to "island hop" in the South Pacific. "Island-hopping" was a military strategy to first invade and liberate the surrounding Japanese-held islands before invading mainland Japan. Month after month, under a hail of bullets and grenades, American soldiers and sailors stormed successive beachheads, where the sands turned red from the blood of dead and mutilated comrades.

The last major battle of World War II was fought on one of these South Pacific islands, Okinawa, which is generally acknowledged to have been the bloodiest battle of the war. The second to last battle of WWII was on the island of Iwo Jima. It is generally acknowledged to have been the second bloodiest battle. Over the course of weeks and months, American soldiers fought to occupy these islands—climbing over bodies of dead soldiers, dodging enemy flame-throwers, mortars, and bullets.

Grier lived in a foxhole and tent on Iwo Jima for five months, as the battle for the island raged and ebbed. He buried the bodies of friends he had fought alongside, handling their severed arms, legs, and heads. After the battles of Iwo Jima and Okinawa, President Truman ended World War II by dropping two atomic bombs on Japan.

When the war was over, after years of separation, Grier returned home to Louise. Louise remembers, "Grier was a changed man. . . . He weighed two hundred pounds when he left, and he weighed one hundred and twenty-nine when he came home. Today we would say he suffered from post-traumatic stress disorder, although nobody called it that back then. . . . He was still a loving person, but he seemed sad a lot of the time. And for the rest of his life, he had flashbacks . . . he would awake in the middle of the night, shaking with nightmares. . . . Of course, I knew I was just lucky he came home alive at all, when so many men had died in the war."

Blacklisted

Trying to resume a normal life in Dallas, Grier started a job with the Veterans' Administration. Then, as Louise tells it, "After serving his country selflessly, his country kicked him in the teeth." Grier was fired because he was labeled a "security risk" and "blacklisted." At the time, Senator Joseph McCarthy of Wisconsin was capitalizing on America's post-war fear of communism by instituting the House Un-American Activities Committee in the U.S. House of Representatives. He recklessly investigated alleged communists and pilloried them in the media and in Senate hearings, so the public could carry out the intention of McCarthy's blacklist by shunning and censuring these people.

A person who was blacklisted was virtually unemployable. In fact, an employer willing to employ a blacklisted person could suffer in the business community. Senator McCarthy's methods were ruthless and vicious. He destroyed peoples' lives and livelihoods with little or no evidence of wrongdoing. With horror, Louise followed news stories of

"I had learned much from that McCarthy nightmare. . . . I learned that innocent people can be accused, and that it is important for some of us to be vigilant about protecting the rights and liberties of the rest of us."

blacklisted people committing suicide because their lives were ruined. She comments, "When you saw the way McCarthy tapped into people's fears, and how people reacted to him and joined the frenzy, you could better understand how someone like a Hitler could ever have come to power. In Dallas, a rabbi and a Unitarian minister spoke out publicly to say that what McCarthy was doing was wrong. They were the only ones. . . . I was so grateful to them— and so impressed by them—that I converted from fundamentalism to the Unitarian church."

Grier was not a communist. Louise believes he was targeted because of some work he was doing with the United Nations, elaborating, "Many people in Dallas in the 1950s considered the U.N. to be a subversive organization. . . . They thought it was a tool of communist agents or that it was on a mission to create one world government, destroying individual national sovereignty." As with most people who were blacklisted, she does not know the actual reason. She says part of her wants to see the FBI files on herself and her husband, but she dreads the re-opening of those old wounds.

Mrs. Grier Raggio, Esq.

Louise and Grier challenged Grier's firing, and eventually he was reinstated. But Louise's dream of being a lawyer's wife and staying home to raise their sons and being taken care of was now put aside for good. Grier suggested to Louise that she go to law school so that they could open their own law practice, and she decided his idea was a good one. "I had learned much from that McCarthy nightmare. . . . I learned that innocent people can be accused, and that it is important for some of us to be vigilant about protecting the rights and liberties of the rest of us."

Additionally, Louise was becoming concerned about her husband's well-being: "He never admitted he was hurting inside, how ravaged—physically, mentally, emotionally—he must have been from the war and the blacklisting. He always put on a brave 'can do' front. . . . That's what men of his generation did. They thought it was 'weak' to complain. . . . In the back of my mind, earning the law degree grew in importance because I could see that Grier was frail. In case he were to become unable to work, I wanted to have a marketable trade I could use to raise our boys."

She attended Southern Methodist University Law School at night, so her husband could be at home with the children after work. They could not afford a babysitter. ("We were dirt poor," she recalls. "We didn't have a phone, a refrigerator, or a dishwasher.") She recounts, "I was the only woman in my class. . . . They didn't want me there. . . . People in the admissions office told me I was taking the place of a man who could use a law degree to support his family. But that's why I was there! I needed to have a way to support my family, too."

Five years later, Louise was awarded her law degree. Her degree read "Mrs. Grier Raggio." There were only a handful of women who were lawyers in Dallas, and law firms openly stated that they would not hire female attorneys. Though at first she had a difficult time finding a job, Louise's career got a boost when she befriended U.S. District Judge Sarah T. Hughes (who, years later, swore in Lyndon Johnson as president aboard Air Force One after John F. Kennedy was assassinated in Dallas). Sarah mentored Louise and emboldened her.

Sarah and Louise

Judge Hughes wanted to see a woman as a criminal prosecutor in the all-male district attorney's office, and she wanted it to be Louise. With Sarah's support and assistance, Louise became the first female assistant criminal district attorney in Dallas. "Everyone who ran things thought women couldn't do criminal prosecution," says Louise. "Women were not even allowed to sit on juries, how were they going to argue before them—persuade them? . . . Nonetheless, Sarah called up the district attorney, Henry Wade, and said she was going to keep calling him until he appointed a female prosecutor. He later said he hired me when she asked because he knew you might as well do what Sarah asked you the first time she asked, because she would eventually get her way."

Louise and Judge Sarah Hughes began holding monthly meetings for all the female attorneys practicing in Dallas. The meetings were held in a small room around a table. They encouraged female lawyers to become active in the community, city politics, and bar

"I was the only woman in my class. . . . People in the admissions office told me I was taking the place of a man who could use a law degree to support his family. But that's why I was there! I needed to have a way to support my family, too."

association activities. "If any one of us heard about an opportunity, we called all the others. If any one of us had a problem, we called all the others." She smiles. "Back then it was survival—now it's called mentoring."

The two of them undertook many progressive projects and had many adventures, one of which Louise introduces, with a laugh, as "Our campaign of terror on Republic Bank!" "Sarah called me up and told me to buy stock in Republic Bank," she begins. "I said, 'Yes Ma'am, I'll do it—just tell me now—why am I doing it?' Sarah explained that apparently Republic's president had said there would be no women vice presidents as long as he was there. So we were going to go to the shareholders' meeting to protest. . . . I bought the stock, and six months later, I dressed up, and we went to the meeting. . . . Sarah now owned fifteen shares of Republic stock, and I had twenty-five. . . . We found out they had learned of our plan and appointed two women vice presidents before the meeting . . . so we had to change the plan a bit. . . . I stood up and thanked the bank's officers for appointing the female vice presidents. Then Sarah stood up and said she was furious at them for not having women on the board of directors! Not long after that, Republic and every other bank in the city had a woman vice president or board member."

> "If any one of us heard about an opportunity, we called all the others. If any one of us had a problem, we called all the others. Back then it was survival—now it's called mentoring."

Balancing Act

Shortly after Louise had entered the D.A.'s Office, Grier opened a law firm with the intention that Louise would join him as soon as she gained experience trying cases and established some connections to bring clients to their firm. When she joined Raggio & Raggio, they set up a satisfying professional experience that would serve clients while keeping their children as the top priority.

For instance, in order to make sure they spent time with their sons every-day, one of them tried to get to the office by 7:00 A.M. and leave for home by 4:00 P.M. Sometimes they brought home files to work on after the boys went to bed. Louise still participated in her sons' activities at school and took her turn serving lunches in the school cafeteria with the other mothers. On weekends, she cooked roasts and meatloaf and froze them, to provide home-cooked meals on weeknights. Having her own business gave Louise the flexibility to balance the competing needs of being a competent professional and a good parent.

It was a hard pace, and Louise was making up the rules as she went along. "I was probably one of the first women lawyers to put it together and have a family and a career. . . . Growing up, I could only conceive of three careers for a woman—teacher, nurse, and secretary. I would have loved to have been a jour-nalist, for instance—I took courses and wrote for the high school and college papers—but a woman couldn't get a job in journalism."

> *"I was probably one of the first women lawyers to put it together and have a family and a career. . . . I used to shudder to think what the local headlines would say if my kids ever got into trouble."*

She confesses to having felt great anxiety as a result of her nonconformance with the societal expectations of women at the time: "In the fifties, people said, 'If you're not with your children all day, they'll end up in the detention center.' And I was scared of that. I used to shudder to think what the local headlines would say if my kids ever got into trouble. . . . My own mother used to tell me I was ruining my children by going out to work in an office!

"The only reason I did it is because I felt I had to. . . . Sometimes I used to feel that I had to have Grier in an office with me, where I could watch him and protect him, or he was going to die. I could never say that. . . . I used to just tell people that Grier had been unhappy with government service and we wanted to work together. . . . I still wonder what Grier could have done if he had not been through so much in World War II. He was such a loving husband and father. And he was far ahead of his time where I was concerned. Most men back then didn't want their wives to be 'stars.' . . . But Grier encouraged me in everything I did."

Rewriting the Laws

Although she was licensed to practice law and was a partner in her own law firm, Louise was not allowed to sign a bail bond for a client—Grier would have to sign it for her. Under Texas law, a married woman could not sign a contract on her own, even in the context of professionally representing a client. Additionally, a married woman could not run a business without her husband's consent or control the property she owned before she was married. Louise recalls, "A woman lost her property rights upon marrying. . . . We used to say if you're a minor, a mentally incompetent person, a felon, or a married woman, you have no rights in Texas."

"You can't go through what I've been through and not be a feminist."

Louise vowed to use this frustration as an impetus to change the law for herself and for the women of Texas. "You can't go through what I've been through and not be a feminist," she reasons. She persuaded the president of the state bar association to let her put together a committee to rewrite the law, and then she organized a task force of domestic relations experts who drafted legislation and worked for its passage in the Texas legislature. The new law allowed a wife to run a business and to control her separate property.

Next, Louise spearheaded an effort to write a Texas Family Code pulling together all the various state statutes concerning marriage, custody, family, adoption, and divorce into one cross-referenced source. Contradictory or antiquated statutes were eliminated. It was the first unified domestic relations law code in the world and served as a model for many other jurisdictions that took on the task of writing a unified code. She was the code's principal organizer and drafter; she participated in seminars all over the state to educate lawyers about it.

For the Next Generation

Thinking back, Louise observes, "Being a woman was an advantage when I started practicing law, because everybody underestimated me. . . . But, I was a child of my time. I grew up accepting that girls were not as valuable as boys. I used to 'sweet-talk' to get my way instead of being direct or having a confrontation. I wouldn't do that today though. Girls don't have to do that today."

There is a speech Louise gives when she is invited to speak at schools, which she calls the "I was a nerd" speech. She explains that as a child, "I was heavy and tacky [only wore hand-me-downs] with poor, uneducated, immigrant parents—and lived on a dirt farm in the country." She tells students, "The only way for me to go was *up!*" Then she explains that the only way for her to move up was to get good grades in school. She tells students that doing well in school is the key to having options in your career path. And she stresses, "Don't concentrate on what you don't have. Concentrate on your assets, on your strengths, instead of your disabilities."

Louise believes young women should avoid the kind of piecemeal schooling she received because of her circumstances. She advises female students to focus on their education first, before they consider taking on the roles of wife and mother, saying, "Women in the past didn't accomplish much out in the world when they got married and then had a child every two years."

"We used to say if you're a minor, a mentally incompetent person, a felon, or a married woman, you have no rights in Texas."

She warns young women, "Never think you have it made. That's what the suffragettes thought after they won the right to vote in 1920, and we've had plenty of new battles for equality since that one!" Louise speaks from experience. She was friends with suffragettes Jane McCallum and Minnie Fisher Cunningham, who led Texas' campaign for passage of the Nineteenth Amendment. She met them when she did some volunteer work at the Austin League of Women Voters after college. "I could listen to their stories all day long. . . . I often thought of Jane and Minnie for inspiration during my dark days. . . . They went through a lot . . . they were harassed and insulted for something which seems common sense. Who could doubt today that women have the right to vote?"

"I grew up accepting that girls were not as valuable as boys. I used to 'sweet-talk' to get my way instead of being direct or having a confrontation. I wouldn't do that today though. Girls don't have to do that today."

Louise concludes, "I had some horrible obstacles to overcome, but they made me the person I am today. I have had more than my share of blessings, and I do what I can to help others. . . . As women get more support in their families and communities, get more education, and make more money, things are only getting better for us."

IV.

JAMIE
GORELICK

When Jamie Gorelick told me she has referenced her children's books at meetings, I started thinking about other sources—besides the very desirable advice of a wise parent, teacher, tribal elder, or pioneering woman—from which I draw guidance. And I sheepishly realized I had been doing my friends a disservice by not acknowledging them as the important role models and counselors they are. Here's what I mean:

When I tell a friend I'm upset about something that happened in an important relationship, as we talk over the events involved, I come to realize there is another unarticulated issue brewing underneath the surface that is the real reason for my anger. It would have been much more difficult, if not impossible, for me to dig out of my emotional reaction and clarify the issue on my own.

When I show a draft of some writing to a friend, and she says, "I like it. I remember when that happened," I feel like I'm on the right track. Or when I e-mail a draft to a friend and he replies, "Nope, I don't get it," his fresh set of eyes and honest feedback re-focus me before I proceed.

Those group discussions with ensemble decision-making (which often seem to take place at coffee shops or with take-out food in somebody's living room) help to manage all the different areas of our lives—often with a lot of laughter in the process. Laughter is an important aspect of taking care of each other and helping each other along. Recent topics submitted for deliberation at group functions include: "How can T—— ask for better training at work?" "Do we like Y——'s old boyfriend better than her new boyfriend?" "What the heck is 'success' anyway?" "Should O—— move to London?" "Would M—— like going to law school?" and "What's a good title for that book E—— has been writing about mentoring?"

Jamie Gorelick helped me to realize a broader concept of what comprises mentoring—I hope that you, too, will realize more of the possibilities for inspiration in your own life, just as I've enjoyed discovering some of my own influences.

(Don't forget your friends!)

I t was a first. At Jamie Gorelick's swearing in as deputy U.S. attorney general in 1994 by Supreme Court Justice Ruth Bader Ginsburg, Attorney General Janet Reno commented upon it: "Who would have thought when we graduated law school we would be swearing in a deputy attorney general who is a woman, to serve under an attorney general who is a woman, and sworn in by a Supreme Court justice who is a woman?" Indeed,

Jamie Gorelick

HOMETOWN: Washington, D.C.
BORN: 1950
PERSONAL: Married
(2 children)
PROFESSIONAL: Vice Chair of
Fannie Mae, and formerly
Deputy Attorney General of
the United States
1997 Recipient of the
Margaret Brent Award

the appointment of these three women by former President Clinton to such high-powered posts furthered his goal of changing the composition of government to better reflect the composition of American society.

The deputy attorney general is second-ranking only to the attorney general, who leads the Department of Justice. The U.S. Department of Justice (often referred to as "DOJ") represents the United States in legal matters, focusing on law enforcement and crime reduction. With Jamie as Attorney General Reno's deputy, for the first time in our country's 218-year history, women held the two most powerful law enforcement positions and were running "the largest law firm in the world," as the DOJ is sometimes called.

The wall outside Jamie's office at the Justice Department was lined with photographs of her male predecessors. Five former deputy attorney generals became attorney general, two served as secretary of state, and two were appointed to the Supreme Court. These photographs served as constant reminders that Jamie was a trailblazer in a new era for women. They were also reminders that the upper echelons of power are filled with men who may or may not be receptive to women entering their realm.

Jamie's Law

The deputy U.S. attorney general is the day-to-day manager of operations at the Justice Department, which employs over one hundred thousand people.

He or she supervises investigations and litigation in many areas, including civil rights, civil claims, antitrust, tax, immigration, environmental law, and criminal law, as well as law enforcement agencies like the Federal Bureau of Investigation, the Marshals Service, and the Bureau of Prisons. The deputy attorney general also coordinates DOJ relations with Congress, the president, the judiciary, and federal agencies.

When Jamie was first briefed on her new duties, she learned Attorney General Reno was facing a problem inherent in many bureaucracies. The attorney general ("A.G.") was often presented with issues that were not adequately defined, requiring her to spend valuable time gathering background information, asking questions, and analyzing facts before a decision could be made. Jamie remembers, "I called my predecessor, who warned me that Reno wanted her deputy to do a job that can't be done. . . . I decided my first step would be to serve up issues to the A.G. for final decisions in a crisp and clean way. I wanted to enable the A.G. to do her job of making important decisions and representing the DOJ to the public."

"I have a system of lists, detailing what needs to be done at work and at home—and I always have back-up plans. That's what happens when you put a working mom in charge!"

As Attorney General Reno noted, there were immediate changes under Jamie's management: "She swept in here one day, dressed to the nines, took command, ordered people around like she was a general, but did it in such a gracious way, and I kind of sat there and looked and they told me that was a Jamie Gorelick."

The A.G. and Jamie decided to decrease the number of people reporting directly to the Attorney General and had them report to Jamie instead, giving the A.G. more time for policymaking and public duties. Jamie increased the frequency of meetings among the Department's top officials to make the DOJ more responsive to inquiries. She identified unresolved issues, assessed the ramifications of various courses of action, and forwarded her recommendations to the A.G. for resolution. At Jamie's behest, a systematic review of Congressional testimony by DOJ officials was required, to ensure that follow-up promised to Congress was being provided.

Jamie's knack for streamlining to the heart of issues is memorialized in a gift from one of her former law partners. He gave her a gavel inscribed "Because I said so," which rests on a base inscribed "Jamie's Law." Jamie used this gavel to run meetings, rapping the table to bring order to arguments and to cut through emotional exchanges to the bottom line. She elaborates, "At the end of a meeting, I would say what we need, and I would give deadlines. People need to know what you want and when you want it."

She believes the secret to effective management is organizational skills. "I have a system of lists, detailing what needs to be done at work and at home—and I always have back-up plans." She grins and chuckles, "That's what happens when you put a working mom in charge! So many working women I know are great organizers. . . . When the tasks on a list have been accomplished, I toss the list away. . . . I don't hang onto information I don't need going forward."

As deputy attorney general, Jamie faced a mind-boggling array of issues on any given day. "We used to say to each other, 'If you don't like an issue before you, wait fifteen minutes . . . somebody will give you a new one.'" For example, Jamie supervised the first DOJ gathering of intelligence on how to secure our nation's computer infrastructure against "cyber-terrorists." Terrorist on-line attacks in cyberspace could paralyze ground and air transportation, telephone systems, gas and oil pipelines, medical records, banking, financial markets, and police and governmental operations. Jamie warns, "There has to be a structure in place to protect us against a Pearl Harbor-like cyberspace attack."

She also worked extensively on old-fashioned crime prevention. "I love cops," she says, in her straightforward manner. "This may sound corny, but it is so patriotic—people who come to work everyday willing to die for their community. To me, cops are the very models of public service. My father was an immigrant, my mother from an immigrant family, and they were extremely patriotic and hardworking, so I'm very comfortable with those values. . . . Cops I've talked with, cops on the street, the most experienced, know criminal sanctions are not enough to prevent crime. Cops need to know the kids in a community, and the kids need to know the cops. Communities also have to offer alternatives to hanging out on street corners and getting in trouble. . . I grew up that way. In my community, there was plenty for us to do. . . . Communities have to be places where we can make friends, make a difference, and make a home."

Jamie flourished at the DOJ and talks about her tenure there with unbridled enthusiasm. "Government, unlike some places in the private sector, doesn't have the ability to waste human resources. It is lean and mean. A talented woman will have her talents used to the fullest—and with less prejudice about her functioning effectively in any particular role. Government service lets people show their stuff!"

A Zig-Zag Path

Jamie's career path didn't begin in government. After graduating from law school, she started at a small white collar defense firm in Washington, D.C. Soon after President Carter started the Department of Energy, she served on the transition team for the second secretary of energy, under the direction of Colin Powell. Then she returned to the private practice of law. Later, during the Clinton Administration, she served as general counsel of the department of defense, supervising more than six thousand lawyers. After only one year, President Clinton tapped her for service in the Justice Department.

Varied experience in both government service and the private sector has allowed her to pursue different interests and opportunities. "Career paths don't have to go in straight lines. Getting involved outside your organization makes you more valuable to your organization. If the organization you're working for can't accommodate your involvement in outside endeavors, find another place to work." This is part of the reason Jamie never pursued a high-paying job in a large corporate law firm: "I feared I would have been buried and pigeon-holed." Also, she knew she wanted to have a family and wanted an environment that offered flexibility.

To students mapping out careers, she says, "Make sure you will be challenged everyday and will be learning all the time. You don't want to just tread water. . . . Find your own pace—don't be driven by what those around you are doing. . . . Be open and ready for opportunities that arise. . . . You can't fully plan the most interesting careers." She also recommends downplaying other people's anticipation of obstacles. "I've developed a certain lack of awe through the years, and it's been helpful. I am never daunted when people say things can't be done. I recommend a lack of awe . . . it helps you get the job done."

When Jamie left the DOJ to become vice chair of Fannie Mae (the United States' largest source of home mortgages), her transforming work at the DOJ received bipartisan acclaim. With fans ranging from former President Clinton to Secretary of State Colin Powell, she could be selected as attorney general at some point in her career by either a Democratic or a Republican president.

"Career paths don't have to go in straight lines. Getting involved outside your organization makes you more valuable to your organization. If the organization you're working for can't accommodate your involvement in outside endeavors, find another place to work."

Aware of her professional rank, she observes, "There are still not enough women in senior positions to give young women enough different kinds of female role models. . . . I take seriously my own role as a mentor—not so much my giving advice, although I do that—but just my being there as an example."

The Importance of Family

The primary example in Jamie's life has been her parents. "My brother and I grew up feeling our parents would do anything for us. My parents had grown up poor, so they wanted to give us every possible opportunity. I had so many lessons—every lesson under the sun—piano, guitar, clarinet, glockenspiel, tap dancing, jazz, modern dance, French . . ."

Her parents played complimentary roles in her development. "My mother gave me her empathy and caring for people and her commitment to community and friendship. On any given weekend, one day I could be in a parade with my Brownies troop and another day I could attend a civil rights march. . . . My father gave me an enormous curiosity about the world. And virtually every woman of achievement I know had a father who believes girls can do anything."

As much as she learned from her parents, Jamie is also open to learning from her kids. She and her husband have two young children, a boy and a girl. They started a family when Jamie was in her late thirties, after her career was blooming.

"It's great to be at home and have your kids just treat you like a mom. . . . It leavens even the most serious moment." When Jamie began at the DOJ, her five-year-old son was a Power Rangers fan. She recalls, "One night, he answered the phone when the Department's Command Center—which kept us in touch twenty-four hours a day—called, and said, 'This is the Command Center for the deputy attorney general.' Dan brought me the phone with a trembling hand, saying, 'Mom, Zordon [the Power Rangers' controller] is on the phone!'"

Jamie expands on what she has learned from her children. "I have given up my old hobbies, which were gardening and tennis, in order to hang out more with my kids. . . . So I've learned a lot about *their* hobbies—*Star Wars*, insects, bicycling, and building with Lego. . . . I like reading to my kids. . . . Childrens' books have so many nuggets of truth in them. For instance, I like *The Little Prince* by Antoine de Saint-Exupéry, which teaches important lessons about building your community.

"I've caught myself quoting storybooks at big meetings. One night we had a senior staff meeting at the DOJ, and one of the assistant attorney generals said something like, 'Oh, we *can't* get the terrorism bill passed, and the immigration bill is *hung up,* and the nominations are *such a problem,*' and the first thing that came out of my mouth in response was 'Stop it! You sound just like Eeyore!' . . . Eeyore is the pessimistic donkey in *Winnie the Pooh* stories . . . soon everyone was teasing him that he needed more of a Pooh and Piglet attitude."

Finding a Balance

She observes that societal expectations of mothers have reversed. Working mothers used to have to explain away the stigma of working outside the home. Now it is assumed women will work outside the home while raising a family, and they often have to justify to others the choice to stay home to raise children full-time. Jamie does not like either of these assumptions, preferring to believe that women have choices unencumbered by such expectations. She notes, though, that mothers with careers have a difficult balancing act to perform in fulfilling professional and personal responsibilities, and a supportive spouse can make the sometimes precarious balance easier to maintain.

Jamie gives her husband a lot of credit for her ability to have a successful career while raising a family: "He's more than a supportive husband . . . I have a partner. My husband is my best friend. He knows me well. He says that I have only two states of being—bored or overworked."

"Make sure you will be challenged everyday and will be learning all the time. You don't want to just tread water."

Jamie shares some of the details of her own balancing act. "I'm always thinking about how to create a better balance in my life. I try to be home in the evenings. I can work on the computer at home after the kids go to bed if I need to. . . . My view at the Department was that, with over one hundred thousand people working there, another hour from me at the office could not make a difference. . . . And I try to not work on the weekends . . . or be away from home more than one night a week.

"The balance I have come to in my life might be one that other women would not enjoy, but there are so many different balances that can work. Everyone has to make their own decisions about priorities. It is an individual choice. That's what our women's movement has been all about—giving us a choice.

This new world of opportunities for women is chock full of choices. And because Jamie's choices have led to her career advancement and the striking of a personal balance, she is a role model to watch.

V.

SANDRA DAY
O'CONNOR

*In the winter of 1990, when I was in my first few months of work after
law school graduation, I came across a small item in the newspaper that
really shocked me.*

*It read that Justice Sandra Day O'Connor had participated in a
"Women in Power" conference at St. Louis' Washington University, where
she had said that the "paucity" of women in executive positions is rooted in
"blatant sex discrimination and the widespread belief that women are unfit
for power positions." She also noted that, although she was at the top of her
graduating class at Stanford Law School in 1952, the only job offer she got
was as a legal secretary.*

*It was news to me that the first woman to sit on the Supreme Court
had been treated so disrespectfully by her profession when she first entered it!
After all, I was working at a prestigious firm, and I knew I sure wasn't
Supreme Court justice material.*

*At that time, I didn't know Justice O'Connor's background at all, but
I had imagined that she had practiced at some "prestigious firm"—maybe
after having a prestigious clerkship (the Supreme Court?)—and was treated
wonderfully everywhere she went during her professional development, before
she blossomed upon being appointed to the Supreme Court. I just didn't*

know. I hadn't been taught anything about this in school, and I didn't have work experience to speak of. It certainly gave me something to think about.

I photocopied the article ten times and passed it around to the other women who sat near me. Several of their reactions were as strong as my own had been. We talked about the "paucity" of women in power positions—at the firm, at our law schools, in general.

I trimmed the article's edges down to its smallest possible size, covered it with strips of scotch tape (homemade laminating), and put it in my wallet. It stayed there for years. One time a friend putting change back into my wallet saw it and said, "Why don't you throw this away?" But I liked bumping into it from time to time. It was a touchstone of sorts.

Eventually I took the article out of my wallet, but I never lost track of it. I know exactly where that taped-over news item is right this minute— it's paper-clipped to the letter Justice O'Connor sent me after we worked on this chapter.

For most of her life, Sandra Day O'Connor's grandmother could not vote in her home state of Arizona. Women in this country were denied the right to vote on the basis of gender until ratification of the Nineteenth Amendment to the U.S. Constitution in 1920. Today, Justice O'Connor not only votes in national elections with citizens of both sexes, but—as one of nine U.S. Supreme Court justices—she casts votes deciding the most important issues of the day presented to the highest court in the land.

Sandra Day O'Connor

RESIDENCE: Washington, D.C.
BORN: 1930 in Greenlee County, Arizona
PERSONAL: Married (three children)
PROFESSIONAL: Associate Justice, Supreme Court of the United States
2000 Recipient of the Margaret Brent Award

"I have taken voting for granted all my life, but it is something many people's grandmothers never enjoyed," Justice O'Connor reflects. "I have a special interest in the period of women's suffrage and entry into the workplace—the two are intertwined. The amount and the rate of progress is astounding. . . . Even in my own time and in my own life, I have witnessed a revolution."

A Century of Change

In order to understand the extent of the changes that have taken place in the last century, Justice O'Connor believes that first we must have an understanding of the past. "In 1776, Abigail Adams—the wife of future President John Adams—implored her husband, 'Remember the Ladies!' in drafting this nation's new charter. Her plea fell on deaf ears. . . . Our Founding Fathers envisioned no role for women in American government. The Constitution permitted each state to determine the qualifications of its voters, which was essentially the same as denying the vote to women. If the federal Constitution did not give women the right to vote, the states were not going to go out on a limb to provide it."

Justice O'Connor explains that women and men moved in separate spheres in the late eighteenth century, with the commercial, political, and professional realms dominated by men, and the domestic sphere relegated to women. "The two distinct spheres defined by gender were rooted in the belief that women were subordinate to men by nature, almost certainly less intelligent, and biologically less suited to the rigors of business and politics." Women were unable to step outside of their domestic role because of what today's theorists name the "cult of domesticity"—the idealization of a woman's role in the home as wife and mother. It was commonly believed that women's natural character is selfless, gentle, moral, and pure, best suited to art and religion rather than logic. O'Connor continues, "Men, on the other hand, were considered to have been fitted by nature for competition and intellectual discovery out in the world—battle-hardened, shrewd, and authoritative."

"Even in my own time and in my own life, I have witnessed a revolution."

Seneca Falls and the New Women's Movement

The seeds of change were sown in the mid-nineteenth century abolitionist movement, when women took a leading role in northern antislavery communities. O'Connor elaborates, "Women reformers spoke at public meetings, conducted petition campaigns, and sharpened their organizational skills. . . . They eventually used these skills to press for their own rights, especially the right to vote.

"A World Anti-Slavery Convention in London served as a catalyst for the women's movement. . . . The United States' delegation included a number of women, but only the male delegates were allowed to sit on the convention floor. Among the females forced to observe passively from the galleries were Lucretia Mott, founder of the first Female Anti-Slavery Society, and Elizabeth Cady Stanton, wife of abolitionist leader Henry Stanton. . . . Afterward, Lucretia and Elizabeth discussed the irony of women working for the anti-slavery cause, supporting the principle that one man should not be enslaved to another on the basis of his race, yet being denied a voice at the convention because of yet another trait one was born with and did not choose—gender.

"When Lucretia later visited Elizabeth at her home in Seneca Falls, New York, they organized their own convention: a 'women's rights convention.' For two days in July 1848, more than three hundred people gathered—some traveling from as far as fifty miles away, which could be a few days' travel in those days. . . . Elizabeth Cady Stanton inspired lively discussion with her Declaration of Sentiment—eleven points outlining rights for women modeled after the Declaration of Independence. Resolution Nine provided: 'Resolved, that it is the duty of the women of this country to secure to themselves their sacred right to the elective franchise.'"

The women's movement in the United States is commonly dated from the Seneca Falls convention. Word of the convention spread, and women started to organize to overcome their proscribed societal position. "Women had been in agreement about their dissatisfaction with the current state of affairs. Now they developed goals. And they took action to achieve their goals. Additional women's rights conventions followed. . . .

"In 1776, Abigail Adams—the wife of future President John Adams—implored her husband, 'Remember the Ladies!' in drafting this nation's new charter. Her plea fell on deaf ears."

Initially, few women felt as strongly as Elizabeth Cady Stanton about the importance of securing the vote. Issues considered to be more pressing included women's inability to control property and earnings, limited opportunities for higher education and employment, and lack of legal status. . . . Elizabeth won supporters as women realized it would be extremely difficult to correct these iniquities without the right to vote."

Legal Setbacks

The potential for change brought about by the emancipation of former slaves after the Civil War brought the right to vote to the forefront of discussion in parlors and state houses around the country. Justice O'Connor relates, "The suffragettes were hopeful, reasoning, 'If newly-freed black slaves are to be guaranteed the same civil rights as all other citizens, including suffrage, shouldn't women be swept up in the expansion of the right to vote?' Their hopes were dashed, however, when the draft of the Fourteenth Amendment introduced to Congress in 1866 incorporated an explicit gender restriction into the Constitution, saying the vote would not be 'denied to any of the male inhabitants' of a state. Explicitly excluding women from the vote in this amendment meant that another constitutional amendment would be required to explicitly provide women the right to vote."

"Lucretia and Elizabeth discussed the irony of women working for the anti-slavery cause, supporting the principle that one man should not be enslaved to another on the basis of his race, yet being denied a voice at the convention because of yet another trait one was born with and did not choose—gender."

Meanwhile, women trying to enter professions such as law were facing insurmountable obstacles. O'Connor tells of how in 1875, one Wisconsin court ruled that the practice of law was unfit for the female character because exposing women to courtroom life would "shock man's reverence for womanhood and relax the public's sense of decency."[1] She recounts another case of a similar nature that went before an Illinois court in 1869 and eventually all the way to the U.S. Supreme Court

[1] *Goodall's Case*, 38 Wis. 232 (1875)

in 1872: "Myra Bradwell of Chicago studied law as an apprentice under her husband and applied to the Illinois bar in 1869. She was refused admission on the basis of her sex. The Illinois Supreme Court reasoned that, as a married woman, her contracts were not binding, and an attorney-client relationship cannot exist without contracts.[2] The U.S. Supreme Court denied Bradwell's claim that this ruling was depriving her the privileges and immunities of U.S. citizenship. . . . In the Court's decision, Justice Bradley wrote, 'Man is, or should be, woman's protector and defender. The natural and proper timidity and delicacy which belongs to the female sex evidently unfits it for many of the occupations of civil life.'"[3]

Winning the Vote

After years of persistence through setbacks and struggle, the suffragettes were eventually successful in their mission to secure the right to vote for American women. "The suffragettes marched. They petitioned. They met with members of state legislatures to line up support for a Constitutional amendment. . . . Some of their opposition disappeared when liquor interests, which had been very hostile to them, needed to re-channel resources to fend off a prohibition amendment. . . . Women won the right to vote on August 20, 1920, when the Nineteenth Amendment was signed into law. . . . Seventy years had passed since the Seneca Falls convention, and it had been a tough row to hoe. Elizabeth Cady Stanton didn't live to see the realization of her dream. She died in 1902. Luckily for us women today, our female predecessors had far more spunk and spirit than they were given credit for . . . I look up to them."

The Justice muses, "Once you get a flavor of the struggle for women's right to vote, think about this: What was it all for? The suffragettes were jailed, attacked, and divorced in their quest for the American Dream of full citizenship. . . . Now, eighty years later, what will you make of their ideals? Do you use your right to vote? What do you think needs to be done for women to

[2] *Bradwell's Case*, 55 Ill. 535 (1869).
[3] *Bradwell v. Illinois*, 16 Wall. 130 (1872).

reach full and equal citizenship in other respects? The suffragettes' concerns are still pertinent today."

Jumping over Professional Hurdles

Gaining the right to vote didn't immediately remove the obstacles still in place for women seeking to be recognized outside the domestic sphere. "Obtaining the right to vote was not a panacea for working women. Society as a whole still accepted the separate and unequal status of women. . . . For instance, a 1936 Gallup Poll found eighty percent of all Americans, men and women, in agreement with the proposition that a wife should stay at home if her husband had a job."

O'Connor cites very personal examples of the gender restrictions that remained in place even decades after the suffragettes won their battle. "Events in my own life illustrate the continuing struggle that remained for women after the right to vote was won. . . . My parents had a ranch on the New Mexico-Arizona border called the 'Lazy B.' My grandfather was a pioneer. He traveled west from Vermont in 1881 to establish the ranch three decades before Arizona became a state. Growing up, I rode horses, drove a tractor, and fixed fences. I played with dolls, too. . . . I thought I could do anything I wanted. After high school, I was even able to fulfill a dream of my father's: to attend Stanford University. My dad had been forced to give up college plans to run the Lazy B when my grandfather died. . . . I stayed on at Stanford for law school.

"Luckily for us women today, our female predecessors had far more spunk and spirit than they were given credit for . . . I look up to them."

"After graduation, I got a dose of women's reality for that era. The world was not going to be my oyster just yet. . . . In 1952, I interviewed with law firms in Los Angeles and San Francisco. None had ever hired a woman as a lawyer, and they weren't ready to start. . . . My husband and I settled in

Phoenix. I held a job in government and then opened my own firm, next to the local supermarket. My clients were generally people who had problems with their bills or leases.

"Then my babysitter moved to California, and I gave up my practice for five years and stayed home. I say 'stayed home,' but I wasn't home all that much! I ran the Junior League, helped the Salvation Army, volunteered at schools. I was so busy that after five years of 'staying home,' I decided a paying job would make my life easier to manage. . . . I became an attorney with the state attorney general's office, which positioned me to be appointed to fill a vacancy in the Arizona State Senate in 1969. I was elected for two more terms, and my colleagues voted me majority leader."

A Woman of Firsts

After finishing her term as the first woman majority leader in a United States legislature, in 1974, Sandra Day O'Connor was elected to the Maricopa County Superior Court. Five years later, she was elevated to Arizona's Court of Appeals. It was during her tenure on the Court of Appeals that President Ronald Reagan became aware of her. In 1981, he nominated Sandra to be this country's first female Supreme Court justice. She says that support by friends Senator Barry Goldwater (R–Arizona) and Senator Dennis DeConcini (D–Arizona) was instrumental in advancing her nomination in the White House.

"The suffragettes were jailed, attacked, and divorced in their quest for the American Dream of full citizenship. . . . Now, eighty years later, what will you make of their ideals?"

"By the mid-seventies, because of the efforts of persevering women and supportive men, I saw a new public awareness of women's potential. For instance, Justice Brennan empathized with what women had been up against, writing in one decision, 'There can be no doubt that our Nation has had a long and unfortunate history of sex discrimination. Traditionally, such discrimination was rationalized by an attitude of "romantic paternalism" which, in practical effect, put women, not on a pedestal, but in a cage.'"[4]

Justice O'Connor provides another example of the changes brought about by the hundred years of challenge to the system. "See the difference from the case of Myra Bradwell. . . . Here, the Supreme Court strikes down a Utah statute providing that child support is required for girls only until their legal majority at eighteen, while support for boys is required until twenty-one. The state justifies the difference by arguing women mature faster, marry earlier, and tend not to require continuing support through higher education, while men usually require this additional support. The Court rejects this argument and concludes, 'a child, male or female, is still a child. No longer is the female destined solely for the home and the rearing of the family, and only the male for the marketplace and the world of ideas. . . . Women's activities and responsibilities are increasing and expanding. Coeducation is a fact, not a rarity. The presence of women in business, in the professions, in government, and, indeed, in all walks of life where education is desirable, if not always a necessity, antecedent is apparent and a proper subject of judicial notice.'"[5]

> *"Growing up, I rode horses, drove a tractor, and fixed fences. I played with dolls, too. . . . I thought I could do anything I wanted."*

Forging Ahead

Justice O'Connor relishes her experience within this new society created by the labors of so many women. "I am thankful for the opportunity to experience a fulfilling career as well as a supportive family life. Lessons I learn in each aid me in the other. I revel both in the latest adventures of my growing granddaughter and in the legal subtleties of the Free Exercise Clause of the

---

[4] *Frontiero v. Richardson,* 411 U.S. 677, 684 (1973)(plurality opinion).
[5] *Stanton v. Stanton,* 421 U.S. 7, 14–15 (1975).

First Amendment. . . . I pursue—and other women pursue and will pursue—the same goals as men in this society, instead of inhabiting a separate and parallel universe."

Sandra Day O'Connor, the daughter of American pioneers—and a pioneer in her own right—comments, "Some of your paths ahead will be easy to traverse: voting, getting a degree, opportunities for varied careers—this part is well-paved by now, with brick, with stone, or packed, smooth earth. Where this next generation of women will make their mark is in expanding opportunities for women throughout all sectors of the economy and in obtaining more positions of power. Here you will have to start fresh paths, navigate obstacles, sometimes stand your ground.

"Forge ahead!" she laughs, "But—'Remember the Ladies!'"

"Where this next generation of women will make their mark is in expanding opportunities for women throughout all sectors of the economy and in obtaining more positions of power. Here you will have to start fresh paths, navigate obstacles, sometimes stand your ground."

VI.
MAUREEN
KEMPSTON DARKES

After I worked at a job for a while, I was asked to handle projects on my own. Consider the following scenario, representative of some of my experiences.

I am asked to coordinate the preparation of a legal brief for one of the firm's clients. I have a month until the brief is due. I discover, however, a few variables and moving parts, namely:

- *The client's employees find documents, in good faith, which I was previously told did not exist; the documents must be incorporated into the brief mid-way through the project.*
- *The senior partner is a hands-off supervisor. The best time to get more than two minutes of his time is before 9 A.M. (Most of the day he is locked away in meetings or on conference calls.)*
- *The junior partner has a hair-trigger temper. I brace myself to be yelled at about something whenever we meet, so I choose the time of day accordingly. ("Do I feel like being yelled at before lunch or after lunch today?") Sometimes his response to a question is, "You're a big girl, you figure it out."*
- *The senior associate is knowledgeable in the areas of law at issue. He provides legal theories to apply to the facts. He promises the junior associates will be able to find cases to cite as precedent for these theories.*

Time will prove him correct.

• The junior associates are spread too thin. Despite this, they are pulled from their regular workload about once a week to spend a day or two on some emergency project that must go out the door. The two who are assigned to do the research on this brief will not truly focus on it until the week before it is due, when they will be told by the assigning partner to work on it to the exclusion of their other cases. The assigning partner will at that time also pull two or three additional associates onto the case to make sure everything gets done in time.

• The paralegals and secretaries have a bunch of administrative problems—the copying service, the messenger service, the over-time schedule, vacations that have been planned for a year, the color of the cardstock the court requires for the cover of the brief.

• All the people senior to me in the chain of command are male (the client, the senior partner, the junior partner, the senior associate). All the people junior to me in the chain of command are female (the two junior associates, two paralegals, and three secretaries).

• Blend all these ingredients together for a brief. Bake and serve.

This is all by way of saying, school just doesn't teach you about a lot of the real-life issues that come up in the workplace! So imagine (with experiences not dissimilar to the example I played with above) how fantastic it was for me to meet a woman who has broken the mold on managing responsibilities and resources in a large organization. As a result of meeting Maureen Kempston Darkes, my management skills are much improved. I'll be surprised if you don't share with a friend something you read in this chapter. (I'm still telling friends about Maureen's management style!)

"Women buy fifty percent of cars and influence eighty percent of car-buying decisions," Maureen Kempston Darkes asserts. "So why can't a woman run an auto company?"

Maureen Kempston Darkes

RESIDENCE: Oshawa, Ontario, Canada
BORN: 1948
PERSONAL: Married
PROFESSIONAL: President and General Manager of General Motors Canada Ltd., Vice President of General Motors Corporation
1998 Recipient of the Margaret Brent Award

Maureen Kempston Darkes is a leader in the male-dominated automobile industry. In 1994, she became the first female president of General Motors Canada, making her one of Canada's most important business leaders and the highest-ranking woman executive in the history of General Motors ("GM"), one of the world's largest companies.

She learned at a young age that life can bring unexpected change. When she was only twelve, her father died, forcing her mother to work outside the home as a bank secretary to support herself and her three children. "An early lesson was that one needs to prepare for this life because we don't know what it will hold," Maureen shares. Her mother taught her to value independence and education, tools which can help a person succeed no matter what unforeseen obstacles one encounters. Because of advice like this, Maureen credits her mother with the success of her three children—Maureen's brothers both pursued careers in the medical field, while she eventually chose the law.

Maureen attended the University of Toronto, expecting to graduate with a doctorate in history so that she could live the academic life of teaching and researching. As her undergraduate years

"People tell me I have gasoline in my blood!"

progressed, however, she decided that she'd appreciate pursuing a more non-traditional career for women, something which might afford her more of an opportunity to help create history rather than simply learn and write about it. She became interested in the law—she enjoyed its intellectual challenges, and realized that it can be an effective tool for helping others. "I saw lawyers making things happen, creating things of real value. Lawyers are perhaps the most creative group in society—we tend to focus only on the image problem brought about by personal injury lawsuits, but most of the profession is engaged in creating worthwhile projects and opportunities for people." Maureen went to the University of Toronto Law School, and after a brief stint at a law firm, she joined the legal staff of General Motors in 1975.

"There were not very many women in management when I first came to GM," Maureen remembers. "But I think over time people came to respect the fact that I worked hard, I was very serious about my work, and I intended to make a significant contribution to the business." She laughs, "People tell me I have gasoline in my blood! . . . Also, I was fortunate to be noticed by two very progressive senior executives who took a liking to me and took an interest in my career development—Jack Smith (who is now chairman of the board in Detroit) and George Peapples (until recently, vice president of corporate affairs in Washington, D.C.)."

"One needs to prepare for this life because we don't know what it will hold."

Nontraditional Management

Maureen's pursuit of a career path she considered "nontraditional" seems consistent with her approach to working within her career as well. She practices what she calls "management by walking," which means she strolls frequently through corporate headquarters, talking with employees about the work they are doing. Her office has no leather couches or doors or even walls—it is an open workspace with a desk, found at the end of a row of similar cubicles inhabited by fellow employees. She uses a nearby glass-enclosed conference room for private meetings and phone calls. "I like informality and flexibility . . . they are critically important qualities in business today. . . . Sitting out in the open, I know what's going on here. People stop by to chat with me all the time."

Workplace Diversity

When questioned about her goals for her company, Maureen lists some of the points you would expect to hear from any person in charge of Canada's most profitable company, with $42 billion Canadian (about $28 billion American) in annual revenues: Customer enthusiasm and loyalty, product quality, and value. In addition to those attributes which have traditionally measured the success of a company, Maureen cites workplace diversity as an equally important endeavor. "The inherent importance of diversity has got to be recognized. We need a work culture where different life experiences and different perspectives are appreciated, and everyone makes a

"Sitting out in the open, I know what's going on here. People stop by to chat with me all the time."

contribution. . . . I want employees to come to work at General Motors every day saying, 'I make a difference. I contribute to this business.'"

Maureen feels that diversity in the workplace isn't just a social responsibility—it's also smart business. "We should mirror the global mosaic within our own organizations. To do this will give us an enormous competitive advantage globally. Look at the marketplace we serve. It's very diverse. . . . Why wouldn't you want the inside of your company to mirror your consumer marketplace? Because if it does, you'll probably understand your consumers better and will be more successful."

GM includes the goal of workplace diversity in developing business strategies in marketing, community affairs, human resources, and with its suppliers. Maureen explains that GM's television and print media targets women consumers as well as men and depicts women of a variety of ages, lifestyles, professional, and ethnic backgrounds. "I think as more and more business leaders come to realize the absolute importance of diversity, we will see a major cultural change. If I can further that cause, I want to do that."

The Women's Advisory Council

To help encourage diversity within GM Canada, in the early 1980s (while she was still part of the corporation's legal staff) Maureen spearheaded the creation of a very nontraditional sort of entity: the General Motors' Women's Advisory Council. The council is comprised of about twenty employees from all areas of the company, including senior management. Maureen explains that the council was formed because senior management at GM recognized women were facing difficulties in their efforts to become part of the company's mainstream. The council met to identify and to respond to issues women faced in the workplace. Maureen's work on the council brought tangible changes to GM's corporate culture.

> *"We should mirror the global mosaic within our own organizations. . . . Why wouldn't you want the inside of your company to mirror your consumer marketplace? Because if it does, you'll probably understand your consumers better and will be more successful."*

The council identified barriers keeping women from reaching their full potential, including prejudice, lack of effective career path planning, exclusion from networks, and the difficulties associated with career/family balancing. To assist women in overcoming these barriers, the council developed progressive policies for General Motors to adopt, including a mentoring program, job sharing, and telecommuting. These policies have changed the face of the workplace for both women and men.

The Mentoring Program

The mentoring program assigns, upon request, a more senior person with whom an employee can meet regularly to ask questions and to discuss setting and reaching professional goals. Employees appreciate the support they gain from their mentors, and senior employees enjoy the opportunity to share what they've learned. Maureen believes, "Those women in an organization who have met with some success have an obligation to assist other women coming along. . . . They do this directly, by providing mentoring. They are also doing this more generally by helping to lead changes in our corporate culture and practices—to facilitate the fuller participation of women and minorities. Changing the culture of an organization is a long-term activity, but it is happening at GM."

The mentoring program has also proven to make good business sense, as employees who are satisfied with their career development are more likely to remain with a company.

Alternative Work Schedules

The council also assisted with implementing alternative work schedules. In addition to part-time schedules, GM offers "flex-time," which allows employees to choose the start and end of their workday within certain ranges of time. This enables employees to structure a workday that accommodates personal obligations such as sending children off to school each morning.

GM also allows "job sharing," which means that two employees literally share one full-time job. For instance, one employee works Monday, Tuesday, and then Wednesday just until lunchtime. After lunch on Wednesday, a second employee arrives and works Wednesday afternoon, Thursday, and Friday. Both people work at the same desk, computer, and phone extension, and both are responsible for continuing the same projects and completing the

"I think as more and more business leaders come to realize the absolute importance of diversity, we will see a major cultural change. If I can further that cause, I want to do that."

same tasks. The two employees essentially function as one. Job sharing allows employees to work a part-time schedule and still affords the company continuity within the office. A shared job is covered each workday by one of the two employees assigned to it, whereas under the traditional part-time scenario, if an employee is out of the office, a task or request may have to wait until he or she returns. Thus job sharing is an efficient way for a company to accommodate an employee's schedule while still maintaining business as usual.

Another of the workplace changes brought about by the council was the implementation of telecommuting. Telecommuting permits employees to perform assignments away from the traditional work site, perhaps assisted by a laptop computer, fax machine, cellular phone, or beeper. The amount of telecommuting an employee can do varies with the amount of responsibilities they have that are transportable. For example, some tasks cannot be performed away from the traditional work site—such as work on a production assembly line.

"Experience has shown that when people are given flexibility, they are generally grateful for it, don't exploit it, and do a better job because they are better able to manage the competing interests in their lives. . . . Jobs can get done without spending ten hours a day of 'face time' at the office. Clients and customers are still satisfied and properly served."

Of these alternative work arrangements, Maureen observes, "Experience has shown that when people are given flexibility, they are generally grateful for it, don't exploit it, and do a better job because they are better able to manage the competing interests in their lives. . . . They're happier. . . . Productivity and accountability do not suffer. Jobs can get done without spending ten hours a day of 'face time' at the office. Clients and customers are still satisfied and properly served."

Community Outreach

The council also developed outreach programs to the community. For example, after noting that a disproportionate number of young females drop math, science, and technology courses, thus narrowing their future career opportunities, the council paired up with educators to prepare a video-based career counseling program that encourages high school students to continue developing skills in those disciplines.

A Varied Career Path

The council's Targeting Improved Participation Strategy, which allows employees to try a new position at GM for a six-month period while maintaining the option of returning to their previous position, is an initiative of which Maureen is especially proud. She explains, "For instance, a woman might want to try a short-term manufacturing assignment to ascertain her aptitude for the work and to measure her desire to move into the manufacturing area. But if it weren't for this program, she would not otherwise be pursuing her interest."

Maureen anticipates positive long-term effects from assisting women to pursue varied interests in the company: "The number of women in entry-level jobs is impressive, but the number of women decreases as occupational rank increases. . . . Certainly women are breaking through the glass ceiling that shuts them out of top positions, but it needs to happen more."

"For young women to progress in an organization, they have to develop a broad base of experience from a variety of experiences within the organization. That is how you groom yourself for top positions."

Maureen has advice to offer young women who want to reach positions of power in the corporate world. "One thing I've noticed is glass ceilings are often supported by glass walls that are just as detrimental to women's careers.

You'll never break through the glass ceiling until you crash down some glass walls. When I say 'glass walls,' I mean that for young women to progress in an organization, they have to develop a broad base of experience from a variety of experiences within the organization. That is how you groom yourself for top positions.

"For instance, a woman who works first in a company's financial offices ultimately needs experience in marketing. And if it's a manufacturing business, she also needs to learn how the plant operates. If the company has offices overseas, she'll need international experience on her way up. You need the widest exposure possible to all of the key elements of an organization to become a leader in that organization."

"I can't stress enough to young women that they must learn the way decisions are made within their organization. When you understand the decision-making process in your organization, you can then influence the process and the decisions."

An example of varied learning is presented in Maureen's own career. "I went to New York City in 1985 for two years to work on GM's divestiture of its South African operations. General Motors had agreed to divest its operations in South Africa in response to anti-apartheid pressure. My job was to find the most expeditious, least costly approach to do that. It was a huge and very complicated endeavor. And that's when I stopped being perceived in the company as just a lawyer and was seen as someone who could move to higher corporate levels and take on much more."

Maureen also urges women to learn the ins and outs of the organization for which they work. "I can't stress enough to young women that they must learn the way decisions are made within their organization. When you understand the decision-making process in your organization, you can then influence the process and the decisions."

In 2000, Maureen was named an Officer of the Order of Canada (Canada's highest honor for lifetime achievement). And if it is true that imitation is the sincerest form of flattery, then proof that Maureen is affecting a great deal of positive change in the business community may be seen in that competitor Ford Motor Company of Canada appointed its first female president, Bobbie Gaunt, in 1997 (three years after Maureen first took the helm at GM). If Maureen Kempston Darkes has anything to do with it, this is just the beginning of a changing mosaic, inlaid with a lot of shattered glass.

VII.
MARGARET HILARY
MARSHALL

I found myself thinking about the Kennedy family a lot as this manuscript took shape. I had to. The Kennedys' dedication to progressive social policies and public service during a dynamic period in American history inspired many of the women I met, including Margaret Marshall.

As a political science major in college, I used to love learning about the Kennedy Presidency (the touch-football games, the appreciation for the arts, those wonderful Cabinet members!). We used the Cuban Missile Crisis as a model for crisis management and political analysis again and again: JFK ignoring the first letter from Khrushchev (the nasty one) and responding to the other (the cordial one); JFK not pushing his opponent into a corner, and allowing his opponent to save face while retreating from the conflict. (Note: I've found that this approach works in regular life, too.)

Margaret Marshall was a teenager in an apartheid-ruled South Africa during the spring and summer of 1963, when the American Civil Rights Movement gained momentum, as African-Americans demonstrated in the streets, boycotted segregated schools, and stood in long lines to become voters.

In June 1963, President Kennedy federalized the Alabama National Guard and committed to fighting race discrimination. In a nationally televised speech, he endorsed a civil rights agenda including legislation to end segregation in public accommodations and race discrimination in employment. Kennedy challenged, "Now, the time has come for this nation to fulfill its promise . . ."

In 1966, Margaret (by this time an anti-apartheid student leader) sat on a platform with Robert Kennedy as he addressed student audiences. Robert Kennedy told students at the University of Cape Town, "I hope you will often take heart in the knowledge that you are joined with your fellow young people in every land, they struggling with their problems and you with yours, but all joined in a common purpose; that like the young people of my own country and in every country that I have visited you are all in many ways more closely united to the brothers of your time than to the older generation in any of these nations. You are determined to build a better future."

Thirty-five years later, I find his words stirring to read. I can't imagine how thrilling it must have been for Margaret Marshall to hear this kind of rhetoric as a participant in the civil rights movement of her country.

Margaret Hilary Marshall explains that as a 1960s college student in Johannesburg, South Africa, "I majored in art history—minored in student protests." Margaret participated in protests as a member of the National Union of South African Students ("NUSAS"), a twenty-thousand-member group that worked to end racism in a country where government rule was based upon racial segregation and white supremacy.

She continues, "Prime Minister Balthazar Johannes Vorster considered

NUSAS to be radical. . . . He called us a red cancer that should be cut out! His government stifled anyone who opposed apartheid publicly. . . . Nelson Mandela was imprisoned, the African National Congress was banned. South Africa was a fine place to be in the mid-sixties if you were white and supported apartheid. Otherwise, it could be a nightmare."

In 1966, NUSAS president Ian Robertson affronted the apartheid government when he invited New York Senator Robert F. Kennedy to address student audiences. As a result, government officials "banned" Robertson; he could not speak in public, study at a university, or meet with students or friends. "Many of the men in the anti-apartheid movement were in prison, or under some kind of restriction, or in hiding," Margaret says. "When Robertson was banned, I was asked to take over as president of NUSAS."

Despite controversy, Senator Kennedy visited South Africa in June 1966 and addressed hundreds of students. Newspapers carried a photograph showing Kennedy speaking at a podium with Margaret seated behind him, next to an empty chair symbolizing Robertson's forced absence.

"Working with NUSAS broadened my horizons," she reflects. "I grew up in the small village of Newcastle, in what is now the Kwa Zulu province, sheltered from the oppressive reality of apartheid. . . . But once I was exposed to that reality, I dedicated myself to campaigning against the apartheid government. As a consequence of my unanticipated leadership role in student politics, I developed new skills, such as how to talk publicly, how to deal with the media—and how to do both in a politically charged arena."

Discovering America

Margaret broadened her horizons further by coming to the United States to pursue graduate studies after college. In April 1968, shortly after her arrival in America, Martin Luther King Jr. was assassinated. "Dr. King's passionate fight for civil rights, without promoting violence, left such an impression on me," she notes. Then Senator Robert Kennedy was assassinated not long after Dr. King. "I had met him just two years earlier when he visited South Africa, so I also felt a great loss at his death. His genuine dedication to the principles of equality was inspiring. King and Kennedy remain heroes of mine to this day."

Although she was now a student at Harvard—halfway around the world from home—Margaret continued her work against racism in the United States.

"Any immigrant can make a difference here. No one in America is born into a situation that it is forbidden by law to change."

She realized her experiences under apartheid in South Africa were a powerful resource she could share in America. Margaret traveled across the United States, continuing her campaign against South Africa's government, arguing that the U.S. government should impose economic sanctions against South Africa and should discourage banks from lending money to the South African government.

She remembers, "I met so many Americans during my travels, from all walks of life. At that time in our history, I found that communities, large and small, were often divided over the great issues of the time: civil rights and Vietnam. I recognized that Americans were conflicted because they were so committed to wanting to do the right thing.

That made a great impact on me. . . . I fell in love with this extraordinary society, a nation that has given me unbelievable opportunities," she smiles, "this society that is in a real sense a society of immigrants. . . . As a result of my protesting activities in America, I could not return to South Africa. At the same time, America opened new paths for me to follow."

"I discovered that in the United States there is a special place for immigrants. Immigrants continue to make the history of this country in new ways and with new energy. Any immigrant can make a difference here. No one in America is born into a situation that it is forbidden by law to change. . . . Once I was committed to staying here, I decided to go to law school. Law plays a central role in this country. We are a nation of laws. . . . Attending law school seemed the best way to learn about American culture and politics."

". . . if you are in the company of people who are good at their jobs, just watch them. . . . Observe how your company's top executives handle themselves in many different ways . . ."

When she graduated from Yale Law School, Margaret began working in a Boston firm. There she discovered that one way to learn new skills was to become a close observer of successful lawyers: "I started to watch lawyers in different situations that were new to me and from which I might learn something. I asked courthouse clerks to telephone and let me know when Boston's best trial lawyers would be giving opening or closing statements in their cases, or cross-examining a key witness. I would then go to the courthouse to watch them.

"More generally, if you are in the company of people who are good at their jobs, just watch them. . . . You don't have to have a relationship with everyone. Observe how your company's top executives handle themselves in many different ways . . . when they interact with the people who work in the cafeteria, or with receptionists; learn from the people who are successful at attracting new clients. . . . Succeeding in your career will go hand in hand with really trying to become the very best you can be."

A Step Forward

After sixteen years in private practice, she returned to help one of the universities she had attended, by becoming the vice president and general counsel of Harvard University—the first woman to hold the post in Harvard's 350-year history. "When I first met with Harvard's president, Neil L. Rudenstine," she recounts, "I did not have any expectation that I would leave my law firm. But, when someone asks you, 'Would you like to walk through this door?' the answer should seldom be 'no.' You take a peek at what it might be like to walk through that door. . . . Take a step or two forward before you decide to reject an invitation. After I learned more about the position, I believed it would be a good one for me. Besides legal issues, the position involved building consensus and reaching compromise on contentious issues—something I've always been good at and I enjoy."

Other factors contributed to Margaret's decision to go to Harvard. "Harvard's president was committed to something I believe in: to excellence and to the university being accessible to the most talented people. If institutions limit or exclude people and their manifold talents, they are weaker institutions. . . . For example, institutional leaders need to focus on how they can bring women along in a way that the women are not constrained by institutional traditions or by their own social conditioning."

She elaborates on her philosophy of how to bring other women along. "Women and others historically excluded from our nation's great institutions of all kinds must be made to feel they now have an interest in contributing to these institutions. One small way that I found was helpful in expanding the numbers of women in civic organizations, such as bar associations, was to take a junior lawyer along to a meeting whenever I could.

"Another thing that helps is to make on-the-job criticism something that is appreciated by the person who receives it, because it allows her to focus on improving some weakness to become stronger. Criticism is often presented in a way that is too personal, and it makes the recipient feel her worth to the institution is diminished or makes her feel isolated from the institution. . . . Whenever I work with more junior women—and men, too!—I am mindful of reflecting on what I've learned in the past and present, and passing those lessons on to them, for better or for worse! I had to learn so much on my own. There is so much to be gained from inclusiveness, and it gives me great pleasure to be part of that."

In 1996, Margaret was appointed to the highest court in Massachusetts, the Supreme Judicial Court, where she now serves as the chief justice. Sitting on the bench is where she feels she belongs: "My respect for an independent judiciary stems from growing up in South Africa, where there was no constitution, no written bill of rights, and where the judiciary could not be counted on to be fair and unbiased. No one thought of going to the courts to redress injustice.

"The Massachusetts Supreme Judicial Court ("SJC") is the oldest court in the United States," she continues. "It pre-dates the Declaration of Independence. The SJC was founded in 1692, but the adoption of the Massachusetts Constitution in 1780 after the war of independence was a key moment in the court's history. It issued the first judgment to end slavery in this country, in 1783, nearly a century before the Civil War. . . . John Adams, who conceptualized the idea of three co-equal branches of government, was a justice on the court. Adams had drafted the Massachusetts Constitution, later used as a model for the United States Constitution. I am a great admirer of John Adams. I served as president of the Boston Bar Association, which he founded." As Margaret (the second

". . . when someone asks you, 'Would you like to walk through this door?' the answer should seldom be 'no.' You take a peek at what it might be like to walk through that door. . . . Take a step or two forward before you decide to reject an invitation."

female to serve on the Supreme Judicial Court and the second female president of the Boston Bar Association) concludes, she starts to grin, "Sometimes I think John Adams is turning in his grave—but Abigail Adams may be dancing."

Sound Advice

Margaret is often approached by girls and young women for counseling on their careers. One piece of advice they seem to find helpful is one she follows herself. "Ask yourself," she begins, "what do you genuinely enjoy doing every single day of your life? Write it all down. What are the things I'm good at? Not good at? What do I enjoy doing? Not enjoy doing? What would I do with my life if there was no pressure from my family or my peers and no need to make money? Ignore the *'shoulds'* of your life . . . the school you *should* attend, the internship or clerkship you *should* pursue. If you read the *Wall Street Journal* or *Barron's* because you should, without any actual interest, you will not be happy as a corporate executive. . . . You don't have to show this list to anyone. Make the list for yourself. Have an honest dialogue with yourself, to begin to think about the kinds of interests you will pursue in your career and your life, and those you will be willing to forego. . . . Re-think and revise the list periodically. You don't have to plot out every move in your career journey by the time you are eighteen or twenty-one or twenty-five years old. . . . Find what resonates within you. The most wonderful thing

> *"Whenever I work with more junior women— and men, too!—I am mindful of reflecting on what I've learned in the past and present, and passing those lessons on to them, for better or for worse! I had to learn so much on my own. There is so much to be gained from inclusiveness, and it gives me great pleasure to be part of that."*

about a career that you find personally satisfying is that your work will be a source of energy for you, not a drain on your energy.

"There are no rules that apply to everyone." Margaret goes on. "Sometimes I advise people to move to a different location to pursue the career they want. For instance, when a young woman tells me she wants to succeed in international affairs, I might advise her to leave Boston and go to New York City or Washington, D.C., where the range of opportunities might be broader. . . . If she tells me she likes the entertainment business, it would probably help if she pursued that in New York City or Los Angeles. If she is interested in the commerce of ideas, she will be happy in Boston—Boston, with its many colleges and universities, is in the business of ideas."

She warns, "Think about the role money will play in your life. When you choose a job, remember that employers paying higher salaries will necessarily make more demands on your time. Usually the equation is 'more money, less control over your time. Less money, more control.' It doesn't take long to learn, but sometimes it does require figuring out . . .

"Sometimes I think John Adams is turning in his grave—but Abigail Adams may be dancing."

"Also, think carefully about the lifestyle you want to have, and balance it against the career choices necessary to support that lifestyle," she recommends. "You may be limiting possible career paths because you are counting on making a certain amount of money. . . . Some people seem to hold on to unfulfilling jobs just to afford the place where they live, or the car they drive, or the watch they wear. Money is not the best measure of satisfaction or success. . . .

"I certainly advise new lawyers to eliminate their student loans and any other debts just as soon as they can—so they can choose from a broader spectrum of career choices, and how they will spend their time, and where they will leave their mark in the world. Some people can't pursue their true passions because they have burdened themselves with far too much debt. . . . I often tease my law clerks about the temptation of money. They know if they come into work wearing too many new outfits when I know they are burdened by debt, they're going to get my lecture on money."

Margaret encourages young women to be honest with themselves about whether they should be in the field they are in, or whether some other calling should be followed. "One of the things I learned about myself by list-making," she says, "is I am more comfortable with the kind of work that resembles a 'chess game,' as opposed to work that requires starting from a 'blank canvas.' Give me a set of rules—say, the applicable state or federal statute—and I'll enjoy working to be as creative as I can within those rules. I'm not an artist or a scientist, with a blank canvas before me, inspired to create from nothing. My way doesn't suit everyone. Some 'blank canvas' people resist the constraints imposed by rules. I thrive in that environment."

> *"Ask yourself, what do you genuinely enjoy doing every single day of your life? . . . What would I do with my life if there was no pressure from my family or my peers and no need to make money? Ignore the 'shoulds' of your life . . ."*

The Question of Gender

To questions about gender in the workplace, Margaret has a sincere response. "I have been noticing gender differences for many years now," she comments. "There are some that you have to fight against—those that involve fairness and equality. Others don't require action. Not every gender difference can be eradicated—or needs to be—to bring equal opportunities in schools and the workplace. But it is always helpful to be aware of differences. . . . For instance, my brother and I were raised together—yet somewhere growing up he learned to do electrical wiring, and I never did. Electrical wiring is not innate knowledge for males. My brother learned to do it along the way perhaps because someone—a parent, teacher, or friend—thought it was important for him to know. No one ever asked me if I would like to learn how to do electrical wiring, but I'm sure I could learn it."

She suggests that there are lots of different ways for women to communicate easily with their male professional counterparts: "I used to be completely out of my depth when men talked about sports. Terms like 'Let's punt!' or 'Monday morning quarterback' used to baffle me. I learned that the sport I called 'football' was 'soccer' to Americans. I wasn't entirely sure who Joe DiMaggio was . . . but I recognized that by talking about sports, colleagues or clients were finding ways to build bridges, common understandings in their work relationship with each other when they talked about things other than work. I looked for other ways to do the same thing. I was comfortable talking about the children in office photographs or travel, books, or movies—and those became my 'small talk' topics.

"I also built confidence in my relationships with colleagues and clients by being accessible to them. I gave people my home phone number. I always inform my secretary about where I can be reached so if anyone is looking for me, she can find me and let me know, wherever I am, at a meeting or having a haircut (and I am confident that she will use her judgment to screen out unnecessary telephone calls)."

"When you choose a job, remember that employers paying higher salaries will necessarily make more demands on your time. Usually the equation is 'more money, less control over your time. Less money, more control.'"

Margaret suggests that it is helpful "to try to make alliances with other women—all women, any woman. Women who advance through levels of power are scrutinized closely. A devastating attack upon a woman's reputation can be the hint or suggestion that other women don't like her or trust her. . . . My generation had to contend with what we called the 'Queen Bee syndrome'— the idea that there is only room for one woman in the group to have any power or position in the whole 'hive' of 'worker bees.' There was always the charge that if a woman is number one, she protects her turf, she won't help other women, and she might even hurt them.

"I have actually never experienced that syndrome. Women ahead of me have always extended a helping hand. But I understand where this perception came from. . . . Women who had careers before my generation achieved remarkable things at tremendous cost to themselves. They were often emotionally spent when they advanced up the ladder—the barriers were so high. They could not possibly have the energy to be supportive of every woman who followed behind. I admire greatly the generations of women ahead of me, and I never experienced them as intentionally exclusive."

> *"I have been noticing gender differences for many years now. There are some that you have to fight against—those that involve fairness and equality. Others don't require action. Not every gender difference can be eradicated—or needs to be—to bring equal opportunities in schools and the workplace."*

She has other observations. "Whenever I'm asked if I'm a feminist, I always answer 'yes,' and then I add, 'I don't know what you mean by that word, and I may not know what I mean.' But I know I cannot disassociate myself from feminism, whatever it may mean. If you are a woman, surely you have to take an interest in issues that concern women in the workplace and in society. If you don't, it will be to all of our detriment."

Women should not think they have to do everything on their own to succeed. She advises, "Reach out for help. You will find that help is there for you. . . . For instance, the first time I needed to prepare a press release, I made a number of telephone calls and asked people to help me until we located one to serve as a model. I've spent a lot of time watching and a lot of time asking. Both are ways to reach out to others for guidance. . . . Asking takes confidence you may have to develop. If you ask, people will help you. If you think asking conveys weakness, you will find it much harder to learn. I have found that if you ask for help and assume people want you to succeed, you will do very well. . . . People will feel included in your progress—they want to see you succeed, not fail."

Margaret recognizes that she is an example to others. She notes, "Anyone can get ahead in this country. I came on my own to the United States with no ties to Boston or to America. I did not come from a home of enormous privilege. I did not know any lawyers here. I was an outsider in every sense. . . . Even if you are an outsider, as I was, with the help of others no barrier is insurmountable. I should know, because so many people helped me!

". . . Try to make alliances with other women—all women, any woman. Women who advance through levels of power are scrutinized closely."

"I hope that I can play the same role for the next generations of women," she states. And she does. A continent away from her days as a South African student leader, Margaret Marshall is still working to tear down the barriers and roadblocks to equality.

VIII.
ELAINE
JONES

As my awareness of gender issues grew, my sensibilities began to change. For instance, I stopped laughing when television or movies exploited stereotypes of women. I began to notice terms like "woman doctor." And notice that you never seem to read of someone being referred to as a "male lawyer," "male executive," or "male basketball coach." This is because in America, the white male is the norm. Given no other information than that someone is "a person," most people think of a white male. So you never seem to hear someone referred to as a "white pilot" or a "white scientist."

It is important to be aware of the way we categorize people. Research has shown that categorizing—things, locations, people—is part of the way our brains process and store information.

I learned that the trick, then, is to be aware of whatever stereotype pops to mind and not to act on it in a way that is biased or unfair. Developing this reaction to stereotypes becomes more important as we become a more diverse, multi-cultural society.

Women of color are twice removed from the white male norm. The intersection of race and gender means that women of color may have experiences similar to white women or to men of color, as well as experiences unique to the group.

On the day I met with Elaine Jones of the NAACP LEGAL DEFENSE FUND, I realized that I had never had the opportunity to have a conversation about career issues with a woman of color who was not one of my peers. (I'll bet this is true for a lot of people.) You might say this is because I don't have enough exposure to diversity in my work experience. You could also say it is because there are just not as many women of color in positions of power and influence as there ought to be.

E laine Jones used public water foun-
tains and bathrooms labeled "col-
ored" during her childhood in the
South, where Jim Crow laws legally
enforced racial segregation everywhere
from buses and trains to hospitals and
the military. Despite the often difficult
environment in which she grew up,
Elaine's parents encouraged her to aim
high and instilled in her a strong sense

of self-worth. "Our dinner table was a training ground!" she exclaims. Elaine's
father was a member of the United States' first African-American labor union
as a Pullman porter, and Elaine's mother was a public school teacher. They both
experienced their share of racial discrimination and worked hard to prepare
Elaine, her older brother, and younger sister for the realities of the world for
African-Americans. "They led spirited dinner-time conversations on segregation, other racial issues, and current events. . . . My parents made us *think*, and
they let us know they were expecting great things of us."

At an early age, Elaine decided she wanted to be a lawyer. She remembers
that her parents encouraged her, but that other adults reacted differently:
"Relatives and teachers used to look sort of sad when I said I wanted to be a
lawyer. I realized when I got older that they had thought it could never happen
for me because of my gender and race, but they didn't want to discourage
me." But Elaine was inspired by the outstanding contributions of African-
American heroines such as Sojourner Truth, Harriet Tubman, Ida B. Wells,
Mary McLeod Bethune, and Constance Baker Motley, and she refused to be
dissuaded from her goal.

After graduating from Howard University, Elaine served for two years in
the Peace Corps in Turkey. Then she approached the challenge that had produced the sympathetic look from many of her elders years earlier. In 1967,
she became the first African-American woman to attend the University of
Virginia ("UVa") Law School. Three years later, she was its first African-

"Relatives and teachers used to look sort of sad when I said I wanted to be a lawyer. I realized when I got older that they had thought it could never happen for me because of my gender and race, but they didn't want to discourage me."

American female graduate. Recently, nearly three decades after her graduation, the University of Virginia awarded Elaine its highest honor—the Thomas Jefferson medal in law.

The handful of women in Elaine's class used to meet in the lounge attached to the women's restroom to support each other, often talking over how to deal with sexist comments and behavior by students and professors. She recalls, "One day during my first week of law school I was taking a break alone in the lounge. A middle-aged white female came in, looked at me sitting on the sofa, and said, 'I know you're on your lunch break now, but when you finish could you clean out the refrigerator?' Then she left. I didn't respond, but I realized she thought I was the cleaning lady! That was a scenario my white female classmates did not have to face." Elaine later saw the woman again in the dean's office—she was his secretary. The woman never apologized for her mistake, and Elaine never discussed it with her, but Elaine carried the weight of the misunderstanding with her for years. "What's surprising to me from my own experience, as well as from stories I have been told, is how small indignities can be very difficult to shake off. You remember them for years, even if you vow to forget them."

Making Choices

When Elaine started law school, she planned to return to her hometown of Norfolk, Virginia, after graduation, to open a general practice law office to help the members of her community. During her last year of school, however, she joined many of her classmates in interviewing for jobs with the large New York City law firms. She eventually accepted a position with what had been

President Nixon's firm, but as graduation approached, she felt concerned about her decision. She started thinking that sometimes the best job and the job that pays the most money aren't the same thing.

"I was taking the job that paid the most money, and I knew it wasn't the job I wanted," she explains. "I felt I had lost my way." Elaine turned to her law school dean, who had become a proven counselor and friend. He helped her to focus on pursuing the kind of work that would be interesting to Elaine, and he helped her to get through the temptation of money. "I had always known I wanted to use my law degree to address social justice issues, so he assisted me in obtaining a position with the NAACP LEGAL DEFENSE AND EDUCATION FUND, INC. ("LDF"). I knew this job would suit me because of the immediate sense of relief I felt when I accepted it."

Elaine joined the Legal Defense Fund in 1970 and, except for two years at a government post, she has been with LDF ever since. Her first few years at LDF were spent arguing death penalty cases throughout the South. The job was enormously satisfying. She recollects, "I was needed. I made a difference to people who were otherwise having trouble getting quality legal assistance—or any assistance." Her work with the LDF opened her eyes to inequities in the application of the law. She offers an example concerning the use of the death penalty in this country: "Application of the death penalty was—and still is—tainted by race discrimination. This

> *"One day I was taking a break alone in the lounge. A middle-aged white female came in, looked at me sitting on the sofa, and said, 'I know you're on your lunch break now, but when you finish could you clean out the refrigerator?' Then she left. I didn't respond, but I realized she thought I was the cleaning lady!"*

has been shown in study after study. . . . For instance, if you look at two homicides committed under similar circumstances by defendants with similar criminal records, a defendant will be several times more likely to receive the death penalty if the victim was white than if the victim was African-American." Thus, Elaine joined the ranks of civil rights attorneys in this country who have developed a tradition of using community organization strategy in court, and public opinion to serve clients and advance causes.

"Decide what you want to accomplish, then work backwards to figure out how to get there. Ask yourself, 'What do I need to accomplish my short-and long-term objectives?' . . . Make six-month goals, one-year goals, five-year goals—and change your goals when what you want changes."

Role Models

Elaine has been LDF's president and director-counsel since 1993, and she is still inspired by her predecessors at the Fund. "The Legal Defense Fund has a glorious history. I have been honored to throw myself into this work, important work begun by LDF's founder, Thurgood Marshall—an American hero—and continued by his handpicked successor Jack Greenburg, who served LDF ably as director-counsel for twenty-three years. Jack hired me as a young lawyer in 1970. LDF's current board cochair Julius Chambers was my mentor while he served as director-counsel from 1984 to 1995. All of us at LDF work hard to live up to the high standards and ideals established by my three predecessors.

"LDF has changed our history and inspired us with its vision of what America could be. LDF asked this country to make good on its promise of equal justice when it led the crusade to have the 'separate but equal' doctrine (the legal basis for segregation) declared unconstitutional in *Brown v. Board of*

Education, which Thurgood argued and the Legal Defense Fund won before the Supreme Court."

Elaine urges others to draw inspiration from the true meaning of LDF's vision of equal justice under the law. "I always tell people, decide what you want to accomplish, then work backwards to figure out how to get there. Ask yourself, 'What do I need to accomplish my short- and long-term objectives? Knowledge? Skills? Formal education? And how will I measure my progress?' Make six-month goals, one-year goals, five-year goals—and change your goals when what you want changes."

Elaine's comparison of attainment of a life goal by laying the precedent for it to the *Brown* decision is particularly powerful when considered against the impact of *Brown:* "The *Brown* decision laid the foundation for ending racial segregation a generation before Southern state legislatures would ever have enacted desegregation legislation. . . . Courts in this country are extremely important and extremely powerful. Consider just two cases: *Roe v. Wade* and *Brown v. Board of Education.* The first decision legalized a woman's right to choose. The second prohibited legally-sanctioned segregation. And each changed American culture radically." The difference in the lives of people before and after each decision illustrates her point. For instance, before *Roe,* abortion was illegal, and women would show up in our country's emergency rooms from the results of self-abortions or illegal abortions. After *Roe,* abortion was legal, and the number of women performing self-abortions decreased dramatically. Before *Brown,* African-American and white children did not attend the same schools, although they might live in the same neighborhoods and play together. After *Brown,* changes came to pass to

"The pursuit of civil rights is not a narrow path to trek," she says. *"Anything that improves the quality of lives and lessens discrimination against African-American people helps society as a whole."*

desegregate America's schools. The holding and reasoning of *Brown* and the 1964 Civil Rights Act were later applied to desegregate other public facilities, including parks, libraries, beaches, and buses.

It's All Related

Through the years, Elaine has believed that discrimination against any group of people is related to discrimination against another group—fighting prejudice in any form will help to break down the barriers that separate all people within society. "The pursuit of civil rights is not a narrow path to trek," she says. "Anything that improves the quality of lives and lessens discrimination against African-American people helps society as a whole." In addition to her fight against racial prejudice, Elaine has taken an interest in litigation concerning discrimination of other kinds—including gender, age, ethnicity, religion, or disability. She refers to the laws governing these protected groups as "sister statutes" because of the interrelationship of the issues involved. For instance, a decision on the admissibility of a certain kind of evidence in an age discrimination suit that is harmful to a plaintiff can also be used against plaintiffs who bring race or gender suits. "Any denial of opportunities to one group affects the rights of other groups," Elaine remarks.

"Be aware that we stand on the shoulders of those who came before us. Remembering them and all they endured for us to get here will help us to proceed successfully."

Elaine believes this interconnectedness between minority groups made the legal theories and energy of the civil rights movement in the 1960s extend to the women's movement in the 1970s. "It certainly was not the case that white women couldn't drink at a public water fountain, attend a public school, or eat in a restaurant. They could go almost anywhere and eat almost anywhere. But—like African-Americans—white women did not have opportunities equal to those of white males. They were limited by societal conventions, and they were judged based upon something they were born with (their gender) instead of on their abilities or the contributions they could make."

Things have changed through the years, but there is still a lot of work to do. "When Thurgood Marshall headed the Legal Defense Fund, litigation was his best chance for making progress in the fight for civil rights. This is because, as I was saying, Marshall needed the courts to take steps society wasn't ready to take. . . . We litigate cases when that is the most effective means toward an end. . . . However, we also engage in advocacy in our institutions—social, political, cultural—which can lead to consensus, action, and positive change. . . . As litigators, it is important that we speak before school boards and Senate committees as well as in courtrooms." It is impressive for the leader of a legal organization that has brought landmark litigation to speak of the important role of alternative means of dispute resolution.

"All of us need opportunities that allow us to show the kind of wonderful and competent people we are. My work is to break down some of the barriers that prevent our merit from being noticed and valued."

A Sense of History

"Be aware that we stand on the shoulders of those who came before us. Remembering them and all they endured for us to get here will help us to proceed successfully. . . . I am often reminded of the African-American families who sent their children to desegregated schools after the *Brown* decision. It tugs at my heart to think those families risked their lives because they believed there is no place for segregation in America. They saw some things we'll never see—and that's a good thing. They changed a way of life, moved this country forward, and made us all better people. . . . We cannot afford to take steps backwards now. . . . We've come too far, it's been too painful, and we've made too much progress."

Elaine points out, "I think it's important for young women to be aware that the Constitution our Founding Fathers adopted in 1787 excluded women. African-American women were arguably twice excluded." The ringing rhetoric of our Founding Fathers—"All men are created equal"—excluded everyone except propertied white males. African-Americans were counted as three-fifths of a person for apportioning congressional seats and were considered chattel, not persons. It was not until the Reconstruction Congress (approximately eighty years later) that the states ratified constitutional amendments making African-Americans American citizens and giving African-American men the right to vote. Gender-based discrimination would still be permitted under the Constitution until the early 1970s (when the work of people such as Ruth Bader Ginsburg began to change that).

"I advise . . . women to be aware of how far we've come over a difficult road, and to help us all continue moving forward by putting themselves into the fray—to pick an issue and participate in our society's evolution. . . . .

Anything you do to improve in some measure the sum total of human dignity is worthwhile. . . ."

Despite all the positive changes in the last thirty to fifty years, the struggle for equality still has a long way to go. "Few people would argue with me," Elaine states, "when I say that we have not yet fulfilled this nation's promise of equal opportunity and overcome our nation's troubled legacy of discrimination." Elaine sums up her mission: "All of us need opportunities that allow us to show the kind of wonderful and competent people we are. My work is to break down some of the barriers that prevent our merit from being noticed and valued."

Fighting Discrimination One Person at a Time

Young women have approached Elaine with their own tales of workplace discrimination. "Certainly exclusion can be explained by reasons other than race and gender, and I don't want to encourage anyone to be paranoid! On the other hand, discrimination is sometimes only evidenced by things like being denied a mentor or important work assignments, or interpersonal slights. In many cases, we'll never know the reason for the lack of inclusion."

Elaine encourages women seeking guidance to have a sense of their history, and to get involved. "I advise these women to be aware of how far we've come over a difficult road, and to help us all continue moving forward by putting themselves into the fray—to pick an issue and participate in our society's evolution.

"I believe anything you do to improve in some measure the sum total of human dignity is worthwhile. There are enough of us who care about progress that some of us can be working on each issue where help is needed—gender, race, poverty, children, the elderly, health care. Pick your issue, and do something positive related to it. . . . What is of paramount importance is to become involved in some cause you care about and to stretch yourself by working on concerns beyond those of your immediate circle."

Elaine has literally dedicated her life to making life better for the rest of us. And she works with an organization that has a tradition of doing the same thing. There are easier ways to make a living. However, she addresses with a smile the unspoken question hanging in the air about all the hard work and all the tough times: "There is a saying—a Swahili warrior song—that life has meaning only in the struggle. Triumphs and defeats are up to the gods. So let us celebrate the struggle."

IX.
HERMA HILL KAY,
NANCY DAVIS, AND
DRUCILLA RAMEY

I have coached high school students in moot court a number of times. I enjoy seeing the students broaden their horizons and develop new skills as they take on a challenge outside of the usual school day.

A few years ago, I walked the halls of the firm where I worked with one of my students. The firm was laid out in an old-fashioned style, with secretaries' offices lining the hallways, and lawyers' offices in an inner layer, virtually hidden, accessible only by first walking through the secretaries' area.

On the way from the conference room to my office, therefore, we saw about ten women sitting in these assorted little outer offices working on the computer or talking on the phone.

The student interrupted our discussion of trial strategy. She said to me, "Don't you have any men lawyers here?"

She actually thought the entire length of a hallway in one of the largest law firms in one of America's largest cities could be filled with only female lawyers! Including women of color!

It was too funny.

This required some quick processing. She was about sixteen years old and a young woman of color. Who could even foresee all of the possible future injustices she might encounter in the workplace or elsewhere because of her gender or the color of her skin? Someday she would have her spirit crushed. I did the equation in my head. I decided it wouldn't be my doing. At least not that day.

So I replied, "The men are on another floor."

She nodded in a matter-of-fact way, question answered. Information digested. We did our work, and she went home. But I couldn't forget the question and the innocent way it was asked. She assumed—even expected—equality and fair dealing. How terrific that she grew up this way! When I was her age, I am positive I never would have thought all those women were lawyers.

I thought of the exchange with this student during the couple of days I spent meeting Herma Hill Kay, Nancy Davis, and Dru Ramey in northern California. In the bold new world these women are constructing, it is possible for that student to be more right than wrong—it is my old-fashioned assumptions that are out of step.

Herma Hill Kay

Very few of America's top law schools include female deans in their administrations. One of the first women to have such a position was Herma Hill Kay at the University of California, Berkeley (called "Boalt Hall"), who served as dean from July 1992 through June 2000.

On the wall of Herma's office hangs a photograph of her with three other women—all wearing skirts, hats, and gloves—all the females from northern California who passed the California bar exam in 1960. There are also framed crayon drawings done by children whose mothers brought them to Herma's classes when babysitters were not available. There is a framed announcement from 1974 for the publication of Herma's textbook *Sex Discrimination,* the first on the topic. She points out a large pink thank-you card from a group of young women who went on to start a public interest law firm after they graduated from Boalt Hall. The room's atmosphere is warm and supportive, reflecting Herma's personality.

The first thing Herma mentions is that she wanted to be a lawyer since sixth grade. In the mid-1940s, she was the only student in her South Carolina classroom willing to argue in a debate that the Confederacy should not have won the Civil War. "My teacher told me I would make a good lawyer. When I told my mother about it, she said 'Don't be silly, you can't make a living as a lawyer—you'll get married.'"

Women in Academia

"In 1919, Boalt Hall became the first major American law school to have a woman on its faculty," she says. "Her name was Barbara Nachtrieb Armstrong. Barbara became a great mentor and friend. She had earned a Ph.D. in social economics from Berkeley. She taught social economics and law in the graduate

Herma Hill Kay

RESIDENCE: San Francisco, California
BORN: 1934
PERSONAL: Married (1 child)
PROFESSIONAL: Law Professor, University of California–Berkeley Law School, Boalt Hall; Dean of Boalt Hall (1992–2000)
1992 Recipient of the Margaret Brent Award

school and was eventually invited to come over to lecture at the law school. . . . The law school was comfortable with her lecturing here because first, she was already a Berkeley professor; second, she was viewed as 'Berkeley's own' and a prize scholar. . . . If she hadn't had those two things going for her and had simply applied to the law school to teach, I doubt she would have been hired in that era.

"When I first started at Boalt, there were not even a handful of women in each entering class. Since then, the percentage of female students here has gone from three percent to fifty-two percent."

"Barbara taught family law and authored a treatise on the subject. It was the definitive work on family law at the time—an academic 'bestseller.' Although Barbara had tenure, she had trouble getting promoted as part of the merit reviews. The dean of the law school then, William Lloyd Prosser, an icon of the legal community (and himself the author of a treatise, the classic *Prosser on Torts*), recognized Barbara's brilliance and wanted to help her. . . . An unconfirmed story goes that he walked to the table where the university's chancellor was eating lunch in the faculty dining room and said, 'No one else here has done this for the school' and plopped down in front of the chancellor the two heavy volumes of Barbara's treatise. . . . Prosser had to resort to unbureaucratic channels because the traditional channels were not responsive," she concludes.

Breaking the One-Woman-At-A-Time Rule

"As Barbara neared retirement, she asked that someone be hired to replace her. And she asked that the new professor be female. I tell people that makes me the law school's first 'affirmative action hire!'. . . So, in 1960—a mere forty-one years after Barbara was hired," she smiles, "the powers that be around here decided we could break the 'one-woman-at-a-time rule.' Boalt then had two female professors! There were only about a dozen of us around the whole country. It was at least another decade before law schools started hiring women as a matter of course."

Barbara played a large role in helping Herma begin her career as a law school professor. "Barbara was a terrific hands-on mentor to me. She gave me her notes from the marital property course she taught. In the afternoons, over tea in her office, she taught me the law of community property. . . . Like her, I always took a special interest in the women students. I wanted to encourage them."

And in time, Herma would coauthor an "academic bestseller" of her own on the subject of sex discrimination. "Ruth Bader Ginsburg, then at Columbia, Ken Davidson of the University of Buffalo, and I met each other at a conference at NYU Law School. . . . Ken told us he had drafted a manuscript for a sex discrimination text. It was written from an employment law perspective. I volunteered to add the family law aspects. Ruth volunteered to add constitutional law, education, and comparative law. Our first edition came out in 1974. After Ruth became a judge, and Ken joined the government, I edited the second and third editions. Professor Martha West, of U.C. Davis, became my co-author on the current fourth edition in 1996 and the 1999 supplement."

". . . In my mind, I think of affirmative action as finding ways to give opportunities to qualified people who might have been closed out of opportunities in the past."

Affirmative Action

Herma discusses some of the changes since those afternoon teas in Barbara's office. "It's becoming a different world. . . . When I first started at Boalt, there were not even a handful of women in each entering class. Since then, the percentage of female students here has gone from three percent to fifty-two percent." Herma believes affirmative action efforts, which increased the number of women and minorities in the student body at Boalt and other law schools across the country, have produced beneficial changes. "Technically,

"Once you open the door of opportunity for a woman who might not have had a certain door open to her in the past, what do you do next? Do you walk away, pleased with yourself that you opened this door for her and leave her to fight it out—to succeed or fail—on a path few others have traveled? Do you try to provide some tools that will help on her journey, or do you go along with her for some or part of her way?"

what's called 'affirmative action,'" she explains, "was a series of civil rights laws, governmental programs, and presidential executive orders by Roosevelt, Kennedy, Johnson, Nixon. . . . But in my mind, I think of affirmative action as finding ways to give opportunities to qualified people who might have been closed out of opportunities in the past.

"For instance, Boalt's admissions policy emphasizes students' individual achievements and places less value on their undergraduate grades and LSATs [the standardized law school admissions test]. . . . Boalt sends recruiters to a wide range of undergraduate colleges, without actually targeting students of a particular gender or race. Our recruiters talk to people, tell them about the school, make contacts with college counselors. In past years, we sent a video about the school to admitted students. We attract a more diverse student body with this approach."

Important questions related to affirmative action are raised by Herma: "Once you open the door of opportunity for a woman who might not have had a certain door open to her in the past, what do you do next? Do you walk away, pleased with yourself that you opened this door for her and leave her to fight it out—to succeed or fail—on a path few others have traveled? Do you try to provide some tools that will help on her journey, or do you go along with her for some or part of her way?"

Helping Others on Their Journeys

Herma has helped many women along unchartered paths—those just starting school, as well as working women who may struggle with a different set of concerns. But all the Boalt women benefited from her work to establish support networks for graduates: "I had the idea for a reunion of Boalt's women graduates, and we had one in spring 1998. . . . Someone was here from every class that had graduated a female student, going back to the 1930s, and up to some women who had been admitted to start that upcoming fall. Over one hundred female alums came to campus for a weekend program including keynote speeches, panel discussions on topics like 'managing your life and your law practice' or 'being a woman of color in the profession,' and of course, social events to get to know each other. . . . Participants thought it was a great success and suggested we do it again in five years."

Nancy Davis, Herma's friend and former student, is a perfect example of the results of Herma's good works. "Nancy was my research assistant. From the start, I was impressed with her resourcefulness, her leadership, and her high ideals. . . . I remember she helped write brochures for college career counselors called, "WANTED by The Law: WOMEN." They helped increase applications to law school from women. . . . She and her friends wanted to start a law firm after graduation to advance women's issues. I helped her to accomplish that because I was drawn to Nancy's determination and desire to help people. . . . One day she told me that while growing up, she and her sisters had a sailboat named *Determination*. I was not surprised!"

RESIDENCE: San Francisco, California
BORN: 1946
PERSONAL: Life Partner (2 children)
PROFESSIONAL: Co-founder and former Executive Director of Equal Rights Advocates, Inc. *1994 Recipient of the Margaret Brent Award*

Nancy Davis

The next morning, at an early lunch, Nancy Davis comments, "I grew up believing the law was an instrument for social change. Herma helped me put that belief into action."

Nancy tells of growing up in a Democratic family in a Republican suburb of Chicago. "An organization called the Young Republicans welcomed people who moved into the neighborhood. Their representative couldn't believe her ears when my mother declined her invitation to join. One of my most memorable moments in high school was wearing a big JFK button on my coat lapel the morning after the 1960 presidential election!"

She recounts, "My dad was a tax lawyer who devoted a third of his time to *pro bono* work and believed deeply in public service. My mother—just about the smartest person I know—was a teacher and homemaker who raised three daughters, all of whom became lawyers. (She would have been the best of all of us!) We all practiced law that reflected their values. My sister Karen, who is deceased, worked with the American Civil Liberties Union in Tennessee and with Legal Aid in Oregon; my sister Linda was chief of the Criminal Section of the Civil Rights Division of the Department of Justice and is now a judge on the Washington, D.C. Superior Court."

In 1965, Nancy went to Mississippi under the sponsorship of the Mississippi Freedom Democratic Party, which was mounting voter registration drives and establishing Freedom Schools in African-American communities throughout the state. "A defining experience for me as a young adult was participating in one of the historic Freedom Summers of the 1960s. . . . I wanted to put my commitment to civil rights into action—I and my sisters, both of whom went to the South in the mid-60s, were acting on the values our parents had taught us. Before we left, our dad sat us down and gave us each a pile of stamped postcards. I remember feeling he was more solemn than usual. He said, 'I know you'll be busy this summer, so don't worry about writing to me and your mother. But drop one of these postcards in the mail to us every-day. If three days go by without our getting a card from you, I'll be on the next plane down there to make sure you're all right.'"

The Influence of Mentors

"Enough about me," Nancy laughs, "let's get to Herma! Herma taught me at Boalt. She was a fabulous role model for women students. She wanted to pre-pare us for the real world. We started a student group called the Boalt Hall Women's Association after Herma called all the women students together and told us that, given the discrimination we would likely encounter as women lawyers, we had better get to know each other and start working together."

Nancy and two of her classmates wanted to start a "teaching law firm" specializing in sex discrimination law. Nancy recalls, "When we broached the topic with Herma, she took us seriously. . . . Herma began providing guidance, and she never stopped. . . . She helped us obtain grants, establish relationships with Bay Area law schools, develop teaching materials, and set litigation pri-orities. She chaired the board of directors . . . She put her exemplary reputation behind us to help us do something we never could have accomplished on our own. . . . Herma taught me the law, while encouraging me to work on improving it to make justice a reality for everyone. One of the greatest strokes of good fortune in my life was meeting and being taught, mentored, and befriended by Herma."

Another key player and mentor in this process was Barbara Babcock, the first woman on the faculty of Stanford Law School (and a 1999 recipient of the Margaret Brent Award). She helped develop the concept of the "teaching firm." Once the firm was open for business, Babcock became the first board president and worked full-time with the firm's co-founders until being appointed in 1976 by President Jimmy Carter to head the Civil Division of the United States Department of Justice.

The Firm

In 1974, Nancy and her colleagues Mary Dunlap, Joan Graff, and Wendy Williams fulfilled their dream of opening Equal Rights Advocates ("ERA"), a teaching law firm. "As a law firm, we represented women's interests in a broad range of cases that included challenging pregnancy discrimination, unequal pay for equal work, sexual harassment, women turned away from firefighter and bus driver jobs because employers regarded those positions as 'men's work,' and unequal terms of incarceration for women prisoners. One of ERA's great strengths has been its commitment to enforcing the outcomes of cases (our lawsuit against the United States Forest Service, for example, went on for nineteen years), to assure that our clients and those they represented reaped the benefits of the risks they took in challenging unlawful discrimination."

"My dream is to see a workplace free of intimidation and harassment of women. I want to see anti-discrimination laws on the books enforced. I want our country to develop sound public policies that reflect the needs of women and their families. . ."

The "teaching" part of ERA gave students from Bay Area law schools litigation simulations based on the firm's real cases. Students also assisted with litigation pending in the firm—researching issues, drafting pleadings, analyzing evidence, preparing for trials. Nancy notes, "Students saw busy courts, anxious clients, and a variety of opposing counsel and judges. They learned about sex discrimination law, but they also learned how to function as professionals in the workplace."

Nancy sums up her goals in starting this firm: "There are enormously complex issues related to this country's policies with respect to half its population—the female half! The movement for women's economic, social, and political equality is still a work in progress," she observes. "My dream is to see a workplace free of intimidation and harassment of women. I want to see antidiscrimination laws on the books enforced. I want our country to develop sound public policies that reflect the needs of women and their families. . . . Ideally, I'd love to see Equal Rights Advocates put itself out of business, because there is simply no longer a need for an organization that fights for these things. But I don't think that's going to happen in my lifetime or the lifetimes of my children."

Toward the end of the conversation, Nancy wants to know who else is being interviewed for *The Counselors*—and seems to either be friends with or at least be an acquaintance of all the women interviewed in the book. She comments, "After two decades of school, work, and networking, finally, we're all getting to know each other!"

Drucilla Ramey

Nancy's good friend Drucilla Ramey is a master networker and the executive director and general counsel of the Bar Association of San Francisco (BASF). Dru (as she is called by friends) encourages women and men to help their careers by getting to know people in the community. "Women and minorities too often think that hard work alone will get you where you want to be." Dru smiles and waves her arms through the air: "I tell them, 'Get out

Drucilla Ramey

RESIDENCE: San Francisco, California
BORN: 1946
PERSONAL: Married (1 child)
PROFESSIONAL: Executive Director and General Counsel, Bar Association of San Francisco
1997 Recipient of the Margaret Brent Award

of your office! Come to the bar association! Your whole life isn't your computer in the cubbyhole on the thirty-seventh floor!' Bar associations sponsor career-enhancing programs, and you'll meet community leaders. . . . Why, I myself met my husband through a prestigious bar association committee. . . . To sit in an office for long hours working hard is a *sine qua non* to career success, of course. But working for the public good with leaders of the legal community can also provide an essential element and an independent basis for self-esteem."

Dru directs the resources of the BASF towards community equality and service. Under her leadership, this large metropolitan professional association with a 110-person staff has presented programs, lobbied legislatures, and submitted briefs in support of issues important to women—including the right to choose an abortion, equal pay for work of comparable worth, gender discrimination, sexual harassment, and breaking through the glass ceiling. She singles out a couple of BASF projects she believes have had the most far-reaching positive effect: drafting and lobbying for passage of a San Francisco ordinance banning discriminatory clubs; and developing and monitoring the implementation of model policies for area employers to adopt, including a Model Policy on Flexible Worktime Options, Goals and Timetables for Minority Advancement, Model Guidelines on Sexual Harassment Policies, and Model Guidelines for Elimination of Sexual Orientation Discrimination. Additionally, Dru has produced videos for national distribution on eliminating discrimination in the workplace and created a national model for community education on breast cancer prevention and treatment.

"With too few exceptions . . . women are still not running things in business, academia, and government. If you look at the raw power in the professions, we're not there yet."

Achieving Equality in Numbers

In terms of sheer numbers, Dru observes that the position of women in the workplace has never been stronger, then continues, "With too few exceptions, though, women are still not running things in business, academia, and government. If you look at the raw power in the professions, we're not there yet."

Affirmative action was a driving force in assisting women and minorities to gain access to professions that had previously been off limits, but not everyone agrees that affirmative action programs were beneficial. Some question whether affirmative action can produce a mentality where women question themselves and doubt they have the ability to earn things in their own right. Dru views such arguments with asperity: "Some would say I have been the beneficiary of what our society calls affirmative action. People of my gender were completely excluded from this profession, then admitted in carefully limited numbers. . . . But white men benefited for a very long time from legally and illegally denying women access to education, to the professions, and to community power. This country is still righting those wrongs. . . . I never heard of a man named Adams, Cabot, Lodge, or Rockefeller second-guessing that his admission to Harvard or Yale wasn't completely merit-based. . . . Women used to not be hired or admitted because of our gender. Now there are people who say women shouldn't want to be hired or admitted or promoted because of our gender—since we might then feel uncomfortable. I say hire me, admit me, promote me—as long as I'm qualified—and if my gender puts me over the top, I'll deal with the discomfort.

"Yale Law School, where I obtained my law degree, systematically excluded women and people of color from its student body and faculty. After dozens of years of limiting women to four or five a year, in 1968—perhaps not coincidentally a year in the middle of the Vietnam War—Yale suddenly admitted

"I never heard of a man named Adams, Cabot, Lodge, or Rockefeller second-guessing that his admission to Harvard or Yale wasn't completely merit-based. . . . I say hire me, admit me, promote me—as long as I'm qualified—and if my gender puts me over the top, I'll deal with the discomfort."

twenty-five women in one year. One of my classmates the following year was Hillary Rodham—before she married Bill Clinton, who was also there. Another barrier was breached in 1968 for racial minorities, until then limited to a few each year—most of whose fathers were either doctors or lawyers or ambassadors to or from an African or South American country." In this newly diverse environment, Dru and her female classmates successfully lobbied the school administration for a women and law course, the first in the country.

An Accomplished Mother

Dru's willingness to suggest doing things that have never been done before and then enthusiastically throwing herself into their development—evident in her lobbying for a women and law course at Yale and again in her work today—is a trait she attributes to her mother. She shares anecdotes about her mother, who pursued a medical career starting in the 1940s with a commitment and resulting success that were rare for a woman of her day.

"My mom titled herself the 'Feminist Endocrinologist' of Georgetown Medical School. Endocrinologists specialize in hormones, and in the early 1970s she received national attention when she responded to a male surgeon who stated publicly that women couldn't be president because of their raging hormonal imbalances. . . . Mom pointed out to him—and it was published in a bunch of newspapers and magazines—that male hormones rage a lot more than female, which makes the lives of males generally shorter and more stressful. She also noted that President Kennedy had had Addison's Disease, which is a hormonal imbalance, yet he had been, for the most part, a fine president who functioned well in a crisis.

"I know the advice my mother rarely hesitates to pass along. . . . First, to pursue your education as vigorously as possible. . . . Second, don't smoke! If you do smoke, quit! My mother is an indefatigable foe of smoking. As a physiologist, she saw what it does to the heart, the lungs, the body. In fact, she says it's practically the only way to defeat the life-enhancing effects of estrogen. . . . At a dinner where Chief Justice Rehnquist pulled out a cigarette, she told him to put it out. As they were later dancing, she smelled the smoke on him and told him—the chief justice of the Supreme Court—that you have to be a congenital idiot to smoke. Of course, she then went on to say, 'But you know, I wouldn't mind if Jesse Helms smoked.'. . . She told me that, to Justice Rehnquist's credit, he was very polite about all this!"

This example from Dru illustrates how dramatically the world has changed: "A few years ago I introduced a medical luminary as the keynote speaker at an awards luncheon sponsored by a law firm founded by a friend of mine. The keynote speaker was my mother, Dr. Estelle Ramey. The firm was Equal Rights Advocates, founded by Nancy Davis. One of the awardees that day was Dean Herma Hill Kay. It used to be that when the director of a big city bar association introduced a parent—a medical professor—to give a keynote address for a firm founded by a close friend, and honoring the 'big cheese' who supported the firm, you'd be on pretty safe ground assuming all four players in that scenario were men. But in this scenario, all the players were women. That could not have happened a generation ago."

"It used to be that when the director of a big city bar association introduced a parent—a medical professor—to give a keynote address for a firm founded by a close friend, and honoring the 'big cheese' who supported the firm, you'd be on pretty safe ground assuming all four players in that scenario were men. But in this scenario, all the players were women. That could not have happened a generation ago."

Because of Drucilla Ramey (and Dru's mother, Dr. Estelle Ramey), Herma Hill Kay, and Nancy Davis, paths that once were hewn out of unchartered terrain and stood alone are now connecting into the highway of achieving women.

X.
JANET
RENO

As I was admitted through security at the United States Department of Justice, I was thinking about when Attorney General Janet Reno first came on the national scene in 1993.

When Reno was nominated to be this country's first female attorney general, I had no less than twenty conversations that day—in person and on the phone—with female friends and colleagues. The gist of all the conversations was this: "A woman as attorney general! Do you believe it? WOW!"

It was big news. Huge. It may not seem like such a big deal now, because we've already had a woman serve as attorney general. And as secretary of state, and in other high-ranking government positions. It's great that it might not sound like a big deal now, or that it might not be when it happens again. But at the time, it was big news.

I was rooting for her.

In 1995, I went to see Reno speak at my five-year reunion from New York University Law School. The school's largest auditorium was packed to capacity. She was a fabulous speaker. I asked her a question from the audience.

And there I was—on my way to ask her a bunch of questions one-on-one. It was surreal!

It brought home to me how blessed I had been in this whole exercise. I was meeting incredible woman after incredible woman—not one of whom I had met or known previously—and being received not like a journalist or a member of the press, but as a person who really could be talked to and trusted. During the course of her tenure as attorney general, it had become evident that Reno was a public servant of the highest caliber. I wanted to learn the stories behind what someone might read about her in the headlines, sensing that her background and motivation could encourage others.

Sure, my friends had been feeling sorry for me lately. Writing this book was requiring an awful lot of time and dedication. I needed to announce more and more often that it would be a "lockdown" weekend, which meant I wouldn't make plans to go to the movies or dinner and unplugged the phone. I would stay home, listen to music, read, and write. (I plugged in the phone for pizza orders.) Lockdown weekends are not good exercise for the cardiovascular system or for the social life, but everything I got out of writing this book meant more to me than any sacrifice.

Feeling like the luckiest woman alive, I was escorted into Janet Reno's office.

I t is a few days before Christmas 2000. Janet Reno is sitting in an armchair facing the fireplace in her office at the United States Department of Justice. Above the fireplace hangs an oil painting of Robert Kennedy, wearing a brown leather bomber jacket. In a few weeks, the Clinton Administration will come to a close, and Janet Reno will no longer be attorney general of the United States.

Reno is the first woman to serve as our nation's attorney general. Traditionally, presidents often have reserved the post of attorney general for a close friend. For example, President Kennedy selected his younger brother, Bobby, and President Nixon chose his law partner, John Mitchell. Although President Clinton did not know Janet Reno personally before nominating her for the post, she became one of the most recognized members of the Clinton cabinet. But today is not about name recognition or how beloved she is by the public. Stories of family, work, goals, and obstacles comprise the agenda for this meeting.

Janet Reno

RESIDENCE: Miami, Florida
BORN: 1938
PERSONAL: Single
PROFESSIONAL: Attorney General of the United States (1993–2001); Highest ranking female ever in a presidential line of succession
1993 Recipient of the Margaret Brent Award

What Attorney Generals Are Made of

"My parents were both newspaper reporters," she says. "My father for the *Miami Herald* and my mother for the *Miami News*. . . . I think you could say I had the kind of upbringing that developed a young woman without some of the societal constraints of the time. That was mostly because of my mother. . . . When I was eight, my mother moved the family to twenty acres on the edge of the Everglades in Florida. Our family needed room to grow, and there she built us the cedar log house I lived in until I moved to Washington in 1993. In our yard, at any given time, you could find an assortment of cows, horses, goats, donkeys, snakes, raccoons, pigs, and peacocks. We called all the peacocks 'Horace.' Alligators lived nearby. My mother was known to wrestle with one once in a while." She grins, "I'm not kidding."

She cups her chin in her palm and leans her elbow on the arm of her chair—emanating accessibility, friendliness, and a willingness to chat. "Even more than four decades later," she continues, "my mother had faith in how well she had built that house. When Hurricane Andrew struck the area, I wasn't sure it was completely safe for us to stay there while ferocious storms were raging. But my mother sat at the kitchen table with her hands folded in front of her—by now she was old and sick—and told me she had built the house well, the house could stand adversity, and we would be fine. Needless to say, she was right. There was massive damage to the Miami area, but all that happened at our house was a couple of the window screens blew out. . . . After the hurricane, whenever I would drive down the driveway through the woods toward home—with a problem, or some obstacle to overcome—the house reminded me you can do anything you really want to if you put your mind to it, and that you can prevail against adversity when you are put together well.

> *"After the hurricane, whenever I would drive down the driveway through the woods toward home—with a problem, or some obstacle to overcome—the house reminded me you can do anything you really want to if you put your mind to it, and that you can prevail against adversity when you are put together well."*

"My mother used to take us deep into the Everglades to meet the Native Americans who had lived there for centuries—the Miccosukees and the Seminoles. They were kind to us, even allowing us to attend some of their tribal rituals. . . . She took us canoeing down wild rivers. . . . She herself once walked over one hundred miles up the Florida coast alone and wrote of it in her journal, 'It might be that someday I shall be drowned by the sea or die of pneumonia from sleeping out at night, or be robbed and strangled by strangers. These things happen. Even so, I shall be ahead because of trusting the beach, the night, and strangers.'"

Reno also lists some more traditional pursuits encouraged by her mother: "My interest in books. Also, she taught me about poetry, and expected me to be knowledgeable about world affairs. . . . We never had a television, though. She used to say that television contributed to mind rot. I think today she would also say it contributes to violence."

She speaks of sometimes feeling embarrassed by her mother while growing up: "With her free-spirited ways, she was so different from other people's mothers. . . . As I matured, I learned to appreciate that she was simply who she was, and it was not for me to judge her or to change her. She wasn't hurting anyone. She loved us so completely! That became more important than anything else about her, and I became comfortable with her just the way she was. I think acceptance of parents and family is a challenge a lot of young people can relate to. . . . .

"One of the things I am proudest of in my life is that I lived with my mother, and when she got sick I was able to take care of her."

"In fact, in my mother's old age, I truly enjoyed walking around Miami greeting people with her—she in her floppy sun hat, smiling without any teeth because she didn't want to wear dentures! . . . Whenever I have asked myself what life was for, or what the meaning of life was, I needed only to look over at her, or call her if I was away from her, or in her last days, reach over and hold her old and gnarled hand to know the answer. . . . One of the things I am proudest of in my life is that I lived with my mother, and when she got sick I was able to take care of her. She was able to stay at home and not go to a nursing home. I tried to contribute to giving her a full, wonderful old age— taking her for rides up and down the river in our boat, despite the fact that she was terminally ill and increasingly frail."

Divine Timing

Janet Reno was a high school debating champion, earned a degree in chemistry from Cornell University, then graduated from Harvard Law School in 1963. She recalls, "My mother kept selling acres of land to pay for our tuition. The family land is now one quarter its original size." In the course of her career, Reno worked in private practice (she was one of the first women to be a partner at Miami's largest law firm), served as the staff director for the Judiciary Committee of Florida's House of Representatives, and was elected state attorney for Dade County (which includes Miami) for five terms, totaling fifteen years. She cites Sandy D'Alemberte (a past American Bar Association president) as a mentor and positive influence in her career development.

The telephone call from President Clinton asking her to be his attorney general could be characterised as "divine timing": "The President called six weeks after my mother passed away . . . I would not have left Miami if she was still suffering with lung cancer." Reno had been approached continually to run for governor or to accept an appointment to the Florida Supreme Court during her mother's illness, but she was not willing to leave Miami and the family's log house until her mother's struggle was over.

The Influence of Role Models

In the spring of 1993, as Reno was learning the ropes of her new job as attorney general, a traumatic event occurred. When she was sworn in, the Federal Bureau of Investigation ("FBI") was in the midst of a three-week stand-off with the Branch Davidians in Waco, Texas. The Branch Davidians were a religious cult with an illegal arsenal of weapons to use against citizens or government officials. Reno approved the FBI's plan to end the stand-off by allowing the use of force and refused to attribute responsibility to anyone but herself for the manner in which the attack was conducted or the fire and deaths related to it. She mitigated a situation that was becoming wrought with finger-pointing and assessment of blame when she stood outside her new office in Washington, D.C., and stated, "I made the decision. . . . I'm accountable . . . the buck stops with me."

Janet Reno's declaration "The buck stops with me" echoes the words of one of her heroes, President Harry Truman, who kept a sign on his desk in the Oval Office which proclaimed "The buck stops here." It was a recognition that decision-makers and those with responsibility often "pass the buck" to others, a course eschewed by Truman. She names other heroes—Washington, Lincoln, Franklin Delano Roosevelt—and points to a plaque on the wall adjacent to where the Kennedy oil painting hangs. The plaque is entitled "Duty As Seen by Lincoln." It says, "If I were to try to read, much less answer, all the attacks made on me, this shop would be closed for business. I do the very best I know how—the very best I can; and I mean to keep doing so til the end. If the end brings me out all right, what is said against me won't amount to anything. If the end brings me out wrong, ten angels swearing I was right would make no difference."

It is fitting that Reno chose for inspiration the words of a national leader who was vilified in his own lifetime, but—with the perspective afforded by the passage of time—is now regarded as a great moral hero. Again, these are words applicable to her own life. In 1980, while serving as state attorney for Dade County, Florida, Janet Reno's office tried but failed to convict five police officers in the beating death of an African-American insurance executive. Rioting ensued throughout Miami, during which some people demanded her resignation. In the midst of the riot, she visited a community center and met with citizens to listen to why they were angry. She conducted an ongoing dialogue with the African-American community about the circumstances of the case—accepting invitations to speak and to listen at church halls, community centers, and schools.

"I made myself accessible to the community," she remembers. "I was everywhere . . . I kept the doors of communication open and made efforts to communicate directly with communities before I made a decision and to explain decisions to them afterward." In time, she was invited to march in the Martin Luther King Jr. Day parade with the African-American community, during which she was hailed as a hero. It is no wonder she was re-elected four times to the office of state attorney.

"Justice is not served when prosecutors cut corners"

Reno's sense of responsibility, attention to detail, preparedness, and integrity shine through in every aspect of her life. When she discusses law enforcement and prosecution, these traits come through again. She applies the metaphor discussed earlier with regard to character, drawn from her mother's experience—building a house that is structurally sound. She says, in part, "People always ask why prosecutions take so long. . . . I think building a prosecution is in some ways like building a house. When we build a case, we focus on building the foundation well, starting carefully, building it carefully, making sure that we go from a lower-level person to a higher-level person if they are involved, until we ultimately identify all the people responsible. . . . When a person drives by a construction site where work is being done on the foundation—out of sight—that person might conclude that since they can't see walls or a roof, little progress is being made. But we can't nail on shingles until we've laid a foundation, put up the walls, and added the roof.

"If you want to accomplish anything, you must start the day by asking yourself tough questions, and end the day by demanding of yourself real answers."

"If we don't build the foundation of a case solidly," she goes on to say, "all of our other work will be for naught. We must proceed on a case in an orderly manner, building it like a house that will stand the test of time and—if prosecutions result—will withstand the scrutiny of the courts and be upheld on appeal.

"Justice is not served when prosecutors cut corners," she concludes. "We must probe our cases beyond—and to the exclusion of—reasonable doubt. All the while we continue digging. New evidence and new leads may surface. In the end, we must meet the highest standard of all. We must convince twelve people on a jury that a crime has been committed and that the person charged is guilty of the crime. . . . The legal system's demanding standards of proof prevent us from basing our judgments on information that might satisfy onlookers who consider the issue for a moment."

Reno shares her reasoning: "If you want to accomplish anything, you must start the day by asking yourself tough questions, and end the day by demanding of yourself real answers. . . . You gain nothing by lying to yourself. See things for what they are. Only then can you assess whether they are 'good' or 'bad' or whether you want to do anything to change anything."

Influencing the Law

In a later discussion with Kinney Zalesne, a young attorney who worked for Reno, Zalesne observes, "I never before met a person who is as impressive and intelligent as Attorney General Reno, yet so down-to-earth and unimpressed with herself. She knows herself. She is comfortable with herself. It is something to strive for. She brings that wisdom and fortitude to every issue she addresses. . . . I have seen her willingness to make an unpopular decision because she believes she is doing the right thing. Her commitment to evidence and law helps her to withstand criticism, and in the end she is usually right. On some issues, like the nurturing of children as an aspect of crime prevention—besides its humanitarian aspects—she was ahead of her time."

As attorney general—and previously in Florida—Janet Reno focused on developing systems to strengthen communities and to help children grow up in a healthy and constructive environment. While state attorney for Dade County, she helped restructure the juvenile court system and visited local schools to talk with students, teachers, and parents—answering questions about her job, giving out her home number, and telling the children to call her at home if anyone abused them. She comments, "I would rather prevent crime by reshaping the lives of children than any other way."

Reno considers child development and family responsibility to be a critical aspect of law enforcement. "Today, it is common to hear police chiefs and prosecutors talk about 'starting out early' with kids. Decades ago, prosecutors who talked about helping children would be branded and castigated—it was called 'a female approach' or 'acting like a social worker.' But without question, at many points in a child's life, adults can target issues and make a difference. Risky times in a child's life are windows of opportunity for positive change.

"When I was a prosecutor," she remembers, "I would look at pre-sentence reports over and over for places where somebody could have intervened. Often, there were big red waving flags in a file—for instance, the father went to jail, the child had a fever that went on too long untreated, or there was a shoplifting incident at age eleven. Now this troubled child got older and committed a murder and robbery, and we were going to put him away behind bars—because that is what we do in this country with those who commit murder and robbery. But there would be the feeling that this incarceration could have been prevented. I see no reason to wait for a child to be thirteen and in some sort of trouble before we try to help. . . . Every child development expert I've ever talked to says the most formative time in a child's life is from birth to age three. This makes it so important to reduce teen pregnancy and to improve prenatal and pediatric care. . . . When kids get into trouble with the law, we can't just lock them away with their mistakes. As a community, we must care for them and help them to take their place among us. They can begin again —they can learn and work and grow."

In addition to promoting coherent community planning, Reno urged domestic federal agencies such as Housing and Urban Development, Health and Human Services, and the Department of Education to collaborate with the Department of Justice to support community efforts for children. To this end, she spearheaded the creation of the "Safe Schools/Healthy Students" program in 1999, streamlining funds from the Justice Department, the Department of Health and Human Services, and the Department of Education to communities all over America for youth programs.

Domestic Violence
A similar collaborative approach has been taken with regard to domestic violence. Reno notes: "I worked with the Department of Health and Human Services to develop a comprehensive support network for victims of domestic violence, including shelters and referral systems to protect and provide for bat-

tered women and their children." She continues, "Domestic violence used to be a private matter within a family. When it became generally acknowledged as a problem through public awareness, it was only from the criminal standpoint. But now we also look at domestic violence in the way it relates to healthcare, the workplace, and the community. . . . We educate people that beating one's spouse, child, live-in, or parent is not acceptable in a civilized society; that this is not the problem of one race or social class; that the overwhelming majority of the victims are women; that domestic violence is the single major cause of injury to women; that domestic violence is usually the result of a pattern of intimidation and control by the batterer, which also includes threats and coercion; and most importantly, that the victims don't ever deserve this treatment."

In the larger context, Reno believes, "A child who sees his or her mother being beaten is more likely to accept violence as a way of relating to people in life. . . . We can do tremendous amounts of good through conflict resolution programs in schools." She emphasizes, "Most of all, families have to be involved. I find when government approaches citizens and says, 'We want to work with you, we need your input,' a lot more good can evolve from that."

"I would rather prevent crime by reshaping the lives of children than any other way."

Native Americans

While attorney general, Reno employed this approach successfully in initiatives to help Native Americans address and solve problems in their communities. "We issued a policy on American Indian sovereignty and government-to-government relations," she describes, "which means that the Justice Department will respect tribal rights and will consult with tribal leaders whenever appropriate. We held a National American Indian Listening Conference to share ideas on how tribal communities can become safer and healthier. . . . We created the CIRCLE Project [Comprehensive Indian

Resources for Community and Law Enforcement] as a way to assist Native American communities to fight crime, violence, and substance abuse more effectively. The tribes play the lead role in developing and implementing efforts."

Not surprisingly, in light of her childhood experiences in the Everglades, Reno has respect for and an affinity with Native Americans: "I learned growing up that many Native American people had strong, strong democratic traditions that value the wisdom of a tribe's elders, respect women as equal to men, and cherish the children as the future of their nation. . . . Tribal traditions give young people a sense of belonging to something special, a sense of their heritage—the feeling that their ancestors were brave and courageous people from whom they can learn and take inspiration."

Leslie Batchelor, former associate deputy attorney general to Reno, later provides perspective on the groundbreaking work with Native American communities: "This Attorney General has done more to try to improve the lives of Native Americans than any attorney general before her. Not only does she take seriously the federal government's special trust responsibility for Indian tribes, but she has worked to strengthen tribal communities from within. Her respect for tribal sovereignty and her commitment to self-determination have led her to encourage tribal communities to draw upon their own traditions and rely on tribal systems of justice to solve the problems they face. By empowering tribal communities, she increased their ability to improve the well-being of their members into the future. I believe this will be remembered as one of her lasting achievements as attorney general."

"I never forget where I'm from and where I'll go back to."

Looking Back, Looking Forward

Of her tenure in Washington, Ms. Reno reflects, "I have learned how much the work of the Justice Department affects all Americans. . . . Our employees work around the nation and around the world. They catch spies and drug lords and terrorists. They stand guard at our borders. They uphold our liberties.

And around the country, the Justice Department is a full partner with police, mayors, and neighborhoods in the twenty-four-hour world of protecting the public and prosecuting criminals.

"In a wide range of areas, we have made important strides to improve the quality of life for Americans. We have put church-burners behind bars, helped boost minority lending to record levels, and enabled Americans with disabilities to use 911, eat out with their families, and sit next to their friends at movies or stadiums." She laughs, "Can you tell I am very proud of the dedicated women and men I have worked with? One of the things I'd like to do—both while I'm in office and when I leave office—is let the American people know that these people who serve them care passionately about this country, work long hours, and deserve our respect and gratitude."

Janet Reno served as attorney general for nearly eight years—longer than any other attorney general in the previous century. When reminded that President Truman left office and returned to Independence, Missouri, to become "Citizen Truman" again, she remarks, "I never forget where I'm from and where I'll go back to."

XI.
JOAN DEMPSEY
KLEIN

I've been a joiner. In high school, I joined the French club, intramural sports, and the tennis team, among others. I never went home when classes ended at 2:30. In college, I joined the pre-law society, the literary magazine, the speech and debate society, and a few more.

I've also been a leader. I've spearheaded projects or served as an officer in organizations I've joined. And I served as my high school's student council president.

"Relevance, Counselor?" as my friend Jerry says to a lot of my stories. Well, two things.

First, joining and actively participating in organizations is a great way to spend free time, meet other people with common interests, and possibly do some good for others. Organization membership can also help build a résumé or increase career prospects.

And second, while I know what it is to be a joiner and a leader, I have never been a founder. I've never started an organization for other people to join and in which they could become leaders. I have never seen, in my mind's eye, the potential for a group of people to make common cause—and then taken that idea and put it into action, to create an entity that has members and newsletters, officers and conferences, and helps people.

For instance, we all know of those extraordinary people on the evening news who, when they face real tragedy—such as having a child disappear, killed by a drunk driver, or born with autism—address their grief, in part, by starting support groups, advocacy groups, or establishing foundations (The Polly Klaas Foundation, Mothers Against Drunk Drivers, and Cure Autism Now, respectively). And what about those who had the vision and gumption to start Amnesty International, Planned Parenthood, or Greenpeace?

Joan Dempsey Klein has done this "founder" sort of thing three times! Before we met, I spent some time thinking about the attributes I expected such a person to have. She should have a strong intelligence, charisma, and a way of speaking that makes people take note, I thought. In Joan Dempsey Klein, I did find all these things and more.

On June 5, 1968, Joan Dempsey Klein needed to open her courtroom before seven o'clock to perform a gruesome duty. The man to be charged with the murder of presidential candidate Robert Kennedy, Sirhan Sirhan, was about to be brought before her by the district attorney.

The preceding day, Kennedy had been assassinated after delivering his victory speech in the California primary. Some viewed this as an event that altered the course of history, as it appeared he could win the election in November and become president. The country was horrified. His brother, former President John Kennedy, had been assassinated while in office less than five years earlier. The district attorney and several police officers stayed awake through the night to prepare the charges for this arraignment. Members of the Kennedy family were flying in from all over the country to mourn. In this emotionally charged atmosphere, Judge Dempsey Klein presided over the courtroom and set bail at $250,000. She also ruled that Mr. Sirhan would be held in custody in lieu of bail.

Then she had to move on and accomplish other tasks on other cases that day. She says it was difficult, but she did it. Joan Dempsey Klein shares this story in the context of a conversation on how decisions made by judges can change people's lives—affecting their freedom or their pocketbook, among other things. She provides the perspective that no matter how crucial a case is to the parties involved (and it may be the only case in which those parties are ever involved) it is still just one of the cases a busy judge may handle in a week, a year, and a career. Clearly, being a judge is not the sort of job everyone could

Joan Dempsey Klein

RESIDENCE: Los Angeles, California
BORN: 1929
PERSONAL: Married (five children)
PROFESSIONAL: Presiding Justice of the California Court of Appeals, Founder of three organizations to advance women professionally: The National Association of Women Judges, The California Women Lawyers Association, and The International Association of Women Judges
1997 Recipient of the Margaret Brent Award

do. Further, more so in 1968 than today, it was generally not the sort of job that would be done by a woman.

Joan Dempsey Klein has been a judge for more than thirty-five years. The sheer longevity of her career as a female professional is worthy of note. Though it is fairly common to find men who have been judges for thirty-five years, the same is not true for women. It is also fairly common to find men who have had legal careers for more than forty years; again, this is not the case for women. In the future, we know this will not be true. Larger and larger numbers of working women will eventually be judges for more than thirty-five years and will eventually have legal careers for more than forty years. But today, Joan is still a rarity.

Growing Up

Joan came of age during the 1930s, when American societal standards held women to respect and obey their husbands above all others. Joan remembers her mother's relationship with her father: "My mother did not have a say in anything. . . . She had no money of her own—never held a job. . . . I remember grocery shopping with my mother on Saturdays when I was a girl. She and I would go through the market with a cart and select food. After the cashier rung up our total, we would ask the cashier to please wait a moment while we retrieved money to pay the bill. Then we walked outside to the parking lot, where my father was sitting in the car. He doled out the money for the groceries to my mother, then she would walk back into the store to pay the cashier. I used to think, 'Can't he estimate how much money she'll need and give it to her in advance?'"

Joan realized her mother's confidence and self-esteem had been whittled away by ongoing dependence on her father. She observes, "My mother did not have a say in *anything*. She had no money of her own, never held a job. . . . They were not on equal footing in that relationship. My mother essentially took orders from my father."

Not wanting to follow in her mother's footsteps became a motivating force for Joan. "Sometimes a parent can show you precisely the person you don't want to become, the same way a parent can show you precisely the person you aspire to become. . . . Whenever I faced hardship in my education and career, the thought of my mother's life provided me with negative motivation, spurring me onward. I persevered through difficulties because I was scared that if I didn't, I would end up being just like my mother."

Reflecting on it now, Joan acknowledges that it must have been difficult for her parents to raise a daughter who refused to follow the well-established family course of conduct, which included a college education and career for men but not for women. "No woman in our family challenged things the way I did. My parents did not know how to handle a girl like me. . . . My father told me he did not believe in education for women."

So Joan went through college and law school without her parents' financial support, working part-time during school terms and full-time during vacations. On the road to becoming a lawyer, she held jobs as a teacher, a playground director, a lifeguard, a sales clerk, and as a legendary riveter.

"'Rosie the Riveter'—that was me! What a transforming experience. . . . I worked for the Defense Department

> *"No woman in our family challenged things the way I did. My parents did not know how to handle a girl like me. . . . My father told me he did not believe in education for women."*

while the men were away fighting in World War II. I shot rivets into planes. I made my own money, and I made a lot of money. I supported myself. I bought myself a car. When the men came home from the war, all the 'Rosie the Riveters' were sent home. . . . We essentially were told that since the men were home to resume their former place, we should resume our former place."

Joan found giving up a source of her growing independence and self-reliance to be difficult. "With the loss of that job, I lost its financial rewards, certainly. . . . But what is not so easily measured—and is equally important—

is that I lost a source of intellectual stimulation, community recognition of my accomplishments, and personal gratification."

Taking the Road Less Traveled

Joan illustrates with a story of how sometimes what appears to be a detour from a chosen path can turn out to be exactly the sort of course you would have wanted to choose for your development. "While I was a lifeguard at the Y, two girls in the pool asked me to help them practice their swimming strokes because they were preparing to audition for a water show to tour Europe. As I helped them, they explained they had no way of getting to the Hollywood Athletic Club for the audition. They urged me to audition with them, so I volunteered to drive all of us. The way it worked out was a bit awkward! I was chosen to travel with the water show—though both of them were not.

"We presented a large cast of swimmers, divers, and dancers in fabulous costumes, with lively music, just like the MGM extravaganzas starring Olympic swimmer Esther Williams. We traveled with a collapsible pool, diving well, and stage—and lush Hawaiian-style sets. . . . We assembled our trans-portable *Palais de Sports* (Sports Palace) throughout Europe—including Paris, London, Zurich, and Rome. We put on a show each night and went sightseeing during the day."

After traveling with the water show for nearly a year, Joan returned home to continue school. As a result of her experience, she learned a number of things worth sharing with others. "First, I gained an appreciation for physical fitness. You don't have to become an amazing athlete to get benefits from physical fit-ness. It feels great to just take a walk, stretch a little, and take deep breaths. If you participate in team sports, there are additional benefits to be gained. Playing team sports makes you more comfortable competing, which is something with which a lot of females are not so comfortable. Girls are usually raised to get along with others and to bring people together—not to compete. But if you want a career, you'll find it's important to be comfortable with competitive people, with a competitive atmosphere, and to win and lose with grace. People who play team sports know lessons are learned from both winning and losing."

Through her time with the water show, Joan also gained an appreciation for travel. Her confidence increased from getting along day-to-day in different countries—handling different currencies, trying new foods, finding historical sights, and meeting people from varied backgrounds. She advises, "Young people can travel on a shoestring budget, with student train passes and hostel passes, and I encourage it—while you can still stand wearing a backpack and before you acquire a taste for hotels and restaurants!"

Comparing Cultures

Because of her love for travel, Joan eagerly participated in the People-to-People program when she became a judge. People-to-People was started by President Eisenhower to introduce Americans to their counterparts around the world—for instance, American engineers might visit engineers in Scandinavia, or American nurses might travel to meet nurses in Argentina. The first People-to-People excursion for female judges was to China in 1983.

"Playing team sports makes you more comfortable competing . . . If you want a career, you'll find it's important to be comfortable with competitive people, with a competitive atmosphere, and to win and lose with grace. People who play team sports know lessons are learned from both winning and losing."

Joan recalls, "I was struck by the fact that the Chinese government was recruiting citizens to become lawyers. Apparently, when China was ruled by a repressive regime, lawyers and other intellectuals were persecuted—and literally chased away to live in the countryside instead of in the cities. When China began opening itself up to do business with the West, it found that people in government and business from the West expected Chinese lawyers to show up to conduct negotiations and to draft contracts. I learned that lawyers and repressive regimes generally don't mix."

Joan has now traveled all over the world—from Japan to Australia, Scandinavia to Kenya—and she believes that the United States provides the best opportunities for women to succeed. Further, the conditions under which she has seen women living worldwide have convinced her that efforts to advance women will be needed for many years to come.

Organizations for Women

One of the ways in which women have furthered their advancement in this country is by organizing together and making joint efforts. Such organizations can take on issues—supporting candidates for public office, advocating in favor of legislation, or raising funds. They can also provide education and inspiration to members or to the public. They can work to improve conditions or increase opportunities for members, or facilitate professional networking for members. The possibilities are as varied as the different types of people who decide to work together, recognizing that a group working toward a common goal probably has a better chance of success than individual or uncoordinated individual efforts.

Joan knows the value of organizations dedicated to women's advancement and is the founder of three: The National Association of Women Judges, The California Women Lawyers Association, and the International Association of Women Judges.

She was a cofounder of the California Women Lawyers Association ("CWLA") in the 1970s, an organization that, among other things, submitted "friend of the court" briefs in important California cases to support affirmative action and abortion rights, and to criticize discriminatory clubs. Joan worked on the CWLA Judges' Committee. She observed a correlation between women lawyers being in a well-organized group and a rise in the number of women on the bench in California. So she went national, and eventually global. She recalls, "The National Association of Women Judges ("NAWJ") was an idea whose time had come for a number of reasons. . . . Whenever there was a conference for the judges in our state, invariably the ten or so females would get together in a room to compare war stories and search for solutions."

During their gatherings in the mid-1970s, the women discovered they encountered a different set of problems than their male counterparts—problems like male attorneys trying to take charge of their courtroom; male attorneys who insulted female attorneys, clients, and witnesses; and male attorneys who would address female judges as "my dear" rather than with the respectful "your honor." Joan explains, "We reasoned that if we've got so many gender issues to contend with, and we're in California—and California is supposed to be such a progressive place to live—then what must it be like for female judges in other parts of the country?" The group decided to identify female judges throughout the country and invite them to a meeting. Joan volunteered to be in charge of the national outreach.

"Young people can travel on a shoestring budget, with student train passes and hostel passes, and I encourage it—while you can still stand wearing a backpack and before you acquire a taste for hotels and restaurants!"

She hired a couple of interns to locate female judges across the United States. There was no computer database of attorneys, no Internet—not even a directory of judges. The interns were able to identify female judges around the country, with larger numbers in traditionally progressive areas like New York City, Chicago, and Florida. Joan invited all the women they found to a four-day conference in Los Angeles, and more than one hundred women accepted the invitation to a meeting in October 1979.

Telling the story of that first conference, Joan smiles broadly: "Words are not adequate to describe the joy. . . . It was so much fun, such a thrill! We couldn't get enough of each other—sharing our experiences, laughing, crying. Everyone was heard saying to each other, 'How can I help you?' I don't think I slept for four days straight. . . . We had so much to tell each other. We were kindred souls, and we were coming together to form an organization to help each other and to help other women come on board and move forward. As a result of that conference, the NAWJ had one hundred and twenty-five charter members."

Cissie Daughtrey, a long-time friend of Joan's and a charter member of the NAWJ, described the need for the NAWJ and groups like it: "A woman's group has a different set of priorities. We see problems men don't see. And it's hard to get some of these things done through the traditional associations. . . . Joan brings women together. . . . There's security in a network of professional colleagues, and Joan has provided that security to countless women."

> *"Always make time to help another woman along. Even the smallest gestures help those who are finding their way."*

Joan describes some of her activities as a member of the NAWJ. "I was part of the NAWJ delegation to Washington, D.C., to meet with key members of the Reagan administration and endorse the nomination of Sandra Day O'Connor to the Supreme Court. Sandra was one of our charter members. She later asked me to testify before the Senate Judiciary Committee on her behalf. I testified that Sandra was a highly qualified judge and that the step of having a woman on the Supreme Court was long overdue."

Then, in 1989, at the tenth anniversary meeting of NAWJ, it was discovered that there was enough support from women jurists visiting from other countries to form an international group for women judges. In 1991, Joan founded the International Association of Women Judges ("IAWJ")to enable this international community to pursue goals with a unified voice. Presently, the IAWJ has over four thousand members from eighty-five countries.

From advice gathered from her community of female judges, Joan was able to decide upon the following method to deal with male attorneys who called her "my dear" as she sat on the bench presiding over a trial: "I would call the attorney to the sidebar and say, 'You are not displaying respect for this court when you call the judge "dear." You may not respect me, but you must respect the court. There will be no more "my dears" unless you wish to be held in contempt.' Needless to say, no one I said that to ever called me 'dear' instead of 'Your Honor' again."

Joan explains why she found this terminology so offensive: "It's not that I don't ever like to be given compliments or called by endearments. But in a professional context, these things are irrelevant to my competency and can subtract from the image of my competency. The courtroom or a serious professional setting is simply not the place for men to display chivalry to women. . . . Chivalry is about men being the protectors of women. One aspect of sexism is the social domination of women by men. The chivalrous rules of who follows whom or how to address each other reinforce the lesser power of women in society. . . . When I am the judge in a courtroom, the male attorney arguing a case before me is not my protector."

Helping Others

Joan's climb to the top has given her a generous perspective on women just starting out. "Always make time to help another woman along. Even the smallest gestures help those who are finding their way.

"Let me tell you the moment I became a feminist. . . . It was after law school, while serving in the state attorney general's office. I was doing the work of an attorney the next level up, but was not being recognized for it by my job title or by my salary. I had heard people were saying that I did not really need to have my job because I had a husband. One day when the head of the office stopped by, I braced myself, looked him in the eye and explained that I felt my contribution was not being appreciated. I asked for an explanation of why I had not been promoted to reflect the workload I already had. He struggled for words. . . . He did not give me any straight answers. As he left my office, in that instant I knew I had not received the promotion because of my gender. . . . I knew that if I were a man with a wife and children to support, I would have had that promotion already. I pledged to myself to continue to push forward professionally despite unfair roadblocks. And I remember feeling overcome with the awareness that huge improvements were needed in the workplace for all women. . . . So, I promised myself

"I still meet people who feel threatened by strong, intelligent women. But I also meet so many men who have daughters that want careers. This changes the male perspective and the way they see me. We have a common cause. I want great things for their daughters, and so do they."

I would always dedicate some part of my life to helping the women who came behind me."

She points out, "Today, there are more women in college than men. And, it is predicted that in the near future, more women will graduate from college than men. Those college degrees are going to open a lot of professional doors for a lot of young women. . . . It's an exciting time. . . . I still meet people who feel threatened by strong, intelligent women. But I also meet so many men who have daughters that want careers. This changes the male perspective and the way they see me. We have a common cause. I want great things for their daughters, and so do they."

Joan Dempsey Klein, a.k.a. "Rosie the Riveter," is today one of the best justices in California—male or female. Adversity has only made her stronger, and along the way she's helped other women find strength as well. She knows that it's up to the next generation to carry on the work of women's empowerment. "I've come a long way, but we still have a long way to go . . . Get out there and start riveting!"

XII.
PATRICIA WALD AND
JOYCE KENNARD

*The strangest part about graduating from law school was the feeling that
I could go out into the world and do anything. What I mean is, when I
graduated from high school, I didn't feel like I could go out and just do
anything. I felt like I had to go to college. And when I was in college, I
didn't feel like I should be doing anything except doing everything I could
to get into law school.*

*After law school graduation, I had some freedom in choosing which path
to take. A lot of my classmates were making their decisions based on wanting
to keep as many options open as possible. This is what I did, too. For me, it
was a mistake. I wish I would have based my decision on what would make
me happy. But I wasn't courageous enough to do it.*

*And so I've learned (and the stories of Pat Wald and Joyce Kennard will
bear this out) that time and experience can lead you onto a different path—
maybe hooking you right back onto one you rejected, lost, or didn't realize
existed. For instance, people who think they're finished with formal schooling
because they've gotten into the workforce and gotten a little older may come
to pursue education again, to help them in the job market or for personal
fulfillment. Some people revise their plans by deciding to branch out—going
into business for themselves, starting a new career, or delaying retirement.*

People say "life is short." But I say life is long. Too many times, I've seen things work out the way they're supposed to—the way that feels right and fits the big picture—only after some time and struggle.

I've always loved the scene at the end of the movie The Natural *where Robert Redford cracks the baseball out of the park—taking the skin right off the ball, as he was meant to do all along. He gets to where he's supposed to be the long way, the hard way, but he's there. And it's a marvelous achievement, made no less marvelous because he didn't get there quickly.*

Pat Wald and Joyce Kennard are absolutely inspirational real-life role models, who remind us that you don't start where you will end up, you might not get to where you want to go on the schedule you set for getting there, and the process of getting there is worthwhile in itself.

Patricia Wald

Patricia Wald relaxes in an armchair in her chambers at the Washington, D.C. Court of Appeals, thinking about her career path. "I was treading a new path, for sure. It included detours, false starts, plenty of bruises along the way—and a few lucky breaks."

She tells of being raised in a Connecticut manufacturing town by her mother, aunts, and grandparents. She does not remember her father, an alcoholic who deserted the family before Pat was two and was not heard from again.

Patricia Wald

RESIDENCE: Washington, D.C.
BORN: 1928
PERSONAL: Married (5 children)
PROFESSIONAL: Circuit Judge, U.S. Court of Appeals for the D.C. Circuit (Chief Judge, 1986-91), Judge of the International War Crimes Tribunal for the Former Yugoslavia in the Hague
1996 Recipient of the Margaret Brent Award

She recounts, "Being the only child in a household of adults made me mature for my age. And I was always young for my grade in school. I went to first grade at the age of four because there were no daycare centers, and the household relied upon all the adults working. Later, I even skipped from sixth to eighth grades. A fond childhood memory is—you know the way people rent videos today?—I used to go to the drugstore with my aunts on Saturday afternoons to rent a jigsaw puzzle for the family to work on that night. It cost a nickel!"

Pat was an A-student and valedictorian of her high school class. She attended Connecticut College for Women on scholarship. A Pepsi-Cola fellowship enabled her to attend Yale Law School. She graduated in 1951. "In hindsight," she reflects, "it was naive of me and my female classmates at Yale—who never saw a woman faculty member, visiting lawyer, or judge—not to realize the whole professional world would have to change for us to succeed in it."

A Curve in the Road

Only two years after completing her streamlined educational path, Pat put aside the practice of law to start a family. "We had five kids in seven years! . . . In the early sixties, our youngest child went to kindergarten, which meant all five kids were spending some part of the day in school. Then, I slowly began re-entering the work world. Thanks to help from a law school classmate who worked for Robert Kennedy at the Justice Department, I worked part-time with a consultant's contract for the Justice Department. I set up a desk in the den at home and did my work while the children were at school or while they slept. Other projects during that time included President Lyndon Johnson's Commission on Crime in the District of Columbia and the Ford Foundation's Drug Abuse Research Project.

"After a few years," she continues, "I felt the children could manage with my working full-time outside the house. The older children helped take care of the younger ones, and we hired household help. So I got a job in the local Legal Services office. . . . Most of the lawyers handling cases there were ten years younger . . . I was a forty-year-old lawyer, and I had no courtroom experience. This was a big change for me—after always being the youngest one in class and a star pupil. The public interest environment provides tremendous experience very quickly, though. Within a year, I was arguing a case before this Court of Appeals on the right of indigent women to get divorced without paying a fee. . . . Now I should add this. It is a ritual for judges and elders of the bar to lecture those younger that they should devote time to *pro bono* work ('for the good of the public'). But I can personally attest—having done a great deal of work in the public interest, for the poor, the mentally ill, and juveniles—that there is great satisfaction in devoting yourself to causes larger than money and personal reputation."

> *"People always ask me whether there is a secret spring of sensitivity to the plight of women or of humanity that a woman judge brings to the law. And I always answer that at least in some cases I think there is!"*

It was when Jimmy Carter won the 1976 presidential election that a strong focus was placed on making a place for women in a national administration for the first time. As a result of her work with the Justice Department, Pat was appointed assistant attorney general for legislative affairs. Then in the late 1970s, when President Carter announced his intention to increase the number of women on the federal bench, Pat applied and was nominated for a position on the United States Court of Appeals for the District of Columbia.

"An Enemy of the Family"

Pat had a stormy confirmation to the bench in the spring of 1979. She came to see how a candidate's private life is put under a microscope upon nomination for a public post: "My daughter's landlord, my son's high school coach, and my gynecologist were interviewed. . . . I was told by a knowledgeable Senate aide how 'the scandal business' works. . . . Your detractors pin *something* on you . . . just to put your name out there to the public. Then they wait for somebody unknown to come forward with the *real* scandal about you. . . . My detractors could not

"In hindsight, it was naive of me and my female classmates at Yale—who never saw a woman faculty member, visiting lawyer, or judge—not to realize the whole professional world would have to change for us to succeed in it."

find anything in my personal life to criticize and exploit. I was faithful to my marriage, and I didn't do drugs—although I had worked on reports about drug usage. But an article I wrote on the rights of juveniles became a target. In it, I suggested juveniles might have certain legal rights when their interests conflicted with those of their parents. I raised questions, such as 'When can legal status for children begin?' 'When can a child make a decision to choose a school, seek medical or psychiatric help on their own, or make a decision to sign a contract?' and 'Can someone under eighteen be informed enough to vote?'"

"It is a ritual for judges and elders of the bar to lecture those younger that they should devote time to pro bono *work ('for the good of the public'). But I can personally attest—having done a great deal of work in the public interest, for the poor, the mentally ill, and juveniles—that there is great satisfaction in devoting yourself to causes larger than money and personal reputation."*

Much to Pat's surprise, editorials appeared all over the country naming her an "enemy of the family." "A fundamentalist preacher holding a red leather Bible testified against my nomination before the Senate Judiciary Committee, saying I was an instrument of the devil. . . . For those aspiring to public office, I advise limiting youthful indiscretions and to face them head-on when questioned!"

Despite her opponents' search for scandal, Pat's nomination was confirmed, and she was heartened to learn of a hidden ally. She remembers, "Senator Robert Dole (R-Kansas) came up to me after the results of the vote were announced and said, 'My wife [Elizabeth] told me not to come home for dinner unless I voted "yes" for your confirmation today.'" Thus, Senator Dole was able to go home for dinner, and Pat readied herself to take on new challenges as a member of the federal judiciary.

The Nature of Judging

Upon taking the bench, Pat learned things about the nature and power of judges that someone who is not a judge may not realize. "The nature of judging," she explains, "can be isolating and frustrating at times. Judges exercise power, but only within tight limits. You cannot initiate action—only react to what is put before you by litigants. Judges don't reach out and find topics they want to rule on and issue opinions on them. . . . The name of the game in this twelve-member environment is collegiality—creating a smoothly running machine where our differences are tackled on paper. There is no point in showdowns and power struggles with other judges on the court." She smiles broadly, "Judges are like monks—but without the unifying bonds of a common faith! We are consigned to each other's company, with good conscience we address hard questions, and we do not speak about our work outside the walls of this 'monastery.'"

A judge who does not agree with the majority as a participant on a panel of judges may issue their own dissenting opinion to explain differing views. Pat elaborates, "In many countries only one opinion is rendered by a court, whether or not all the judges agree. Minority dissenters are silenced. The rationale for this is that it may be unsettling to citizens and to the development of a stable body of law for judges to disagree with each other publicly. In the United States, however, our practice is different. From the beginning, we have allowed dissenting opinions on the record, to be looked at again with the intelligence of a future day."

Does gender play a role in her decisions? "In most of my cases, my gender does not make a difference . . . but

"A fundamentalist preacher holding a red leather Bible testified against my nomination before the Senate Judiciary Committee, saying I was an instrument of the devil. . . . For those aspiring to public office, I advise limiting youthful indiscretions and to face them head-on when questioned!"

sometimes I see something in a case my male colleagues simply don't get—for instance, my intuitive negative reaction to an asserted, but undocumented, justification that women did not get choice assignments in an agency because they chose not to compete for them. . . . People always ask me whether there is a secret spring of sensitivity to the plight of women or of humanity that a woman judge brings to the law. And I always answer that at least in some cases I think there is!"

Of the present place of women in the workplace, Pat observes, "The majority of women in this country work in gender-segregated jobs without much opportunity for advancement. Sex segregation by occupation is extensive, pervasive, and—it sometimes seems—intractable. Women hold few construction jobs, ninety percent of clerical jobs, and about two-thirds of all the minimum-wage jobs. . . . Women simply have to be given a chance to try their hand at other jobs."

"Young people today are the key players for this country's participation in a global economy. Don't avoid the game. Your work in the several decades when your schooling is over will be the most important part of your life . . . Make it count."

One of the reasons women have been held back from exploring new areas is they are told they don't have "merit" for a job. She asks, "What does it mean to say someone 'has merit' for a particular position? Individual merit is, in the end, a social conclusion—influenced substantially by conventional stereotypes and past traditions. In many cases, only affirmative efforts to assist women—the way President Carter did—can bring equilibrium, so individual merit based on non-gender criteria can prevail over the long run."

Pat suggests investing time in developing oneself as 'human capital.' "In this new millennium," she reasons, "the workplace needs young women with finely-honed skills in marketing, personnel training and management, and computer sciences. And let me toot the horn of the legal profession—lawyers serve as negotiators, dealmakers, advisors, and advocates. . . . Young people today are the key players for this country's participation in a global economy. Don't avoid the game. Your work in the several decades when your schooling is over will be the most important part of your life. . . . Make it count."

Joyce Kennard

A month later, three thousand miles away on the opposite coast of the United States, Joyce Kennard tells a story in her chambers that presents different difficulties than those presented by Pat Wald—yet her story shares the common theme of success borne out of a winding path including obstacles and detours. "I was born during World War II on the island of Java, then a part of the Dutch colonial empire," Joyce starts. "I'm of

Joyce Kennard

RESIDENCE: San Francisco, California
BORN: 1941, island of Java
PERSONAL: Married
PROFESSIONAL: Associate Justice, California Supreme Court
1995 Recipient of the Margaret Brent Award

Indonesian, Dutch, and Chinese descent. My father died in a Japanese concentration camp when I was a year old." She then spent her early childhood in an internment camp with her widowed mother. . . "Shortly after liberation by the Allied troops, when I was about five, a playmate showed me the thickest, most beautiful book I had ever seen. It had thousands of pictures of toys and pretty dresses, things I had never had, things I associated with a fairytale world. It was a Sears catalog!

"Five years later," she continues, "after Indonesia gained its independence from the Dutch, my mother and I left for the last remaining Dutch colony in the East Indies—the western half of New Guinea. My mother found a job as a typist with a Dutch oil company. . . . We lived in a racially segregated area in a small Quonset hut shared with four other families. . . . The bathroom was an outdoor enclosure containing an oil drum filled with water; the toilet was a filthy ditch at the edge of the jungle. . . . I attended a tiny school run by Catholic missionaries. My fellow students were the sons and daughters of natives whose not-too-distant ancestors had been cannibals.

"The school folded when I was thirteen. . . . The only other school was five days' sailing away, so that was where my mother took me," Joyce states simply, as though this remarkable move was the only logical next step. "Then a year later, when I was fourteen, there was no more schooling to be had there. . . . My education had been woefully inadequate, but I had been taught the rudiments of English—and I picked up a lot of simple words related to love and heartbreak by listening to Radio Australia, which regularly played the American top hits. To this day," she smiles, "I can either sing or hum those hits from the early fifties."

Joyce's mother continued to be resourceful in seeking new opportunities to further her daughter's education. "My mother realized that the wild jungles of New Guinea—basically a man's country—was no place for a fourteen-year-old girl. Determined to get me an education, my mother decided we should leave for Holland. . . . In Holland I experienced such wonders as making my very first telephone call and getting my first peek at television. . . . My mother found a job in a restaurant peeling onions. And eventually she talked the director of a high school into accepting me as a student on a trial basis. . . . When the director noted my lack of background in math, my mother pointed out my high grades in whatever subjects the New Guinea missionaries had taught. I was accepted on the condition that I would get special tutoring in math."

But only six months later, Joyce's schooling would come to an abrupt end: "A tumor on my leg led to an operation and then resulted in an amputation above the knee. . . . I knew I could never catch up in school. And there were no second or third chances in Holland at that time." Thus, Joyce learned typing and shorthand and became a secretary at sixteen.

"A couple of years passed. And then around 1960," she relates, "America opened up a special immigration quota for people of Dutch nationality who were displaced from New Guinea when it changed from Dutch to Indonesian rule. My mother and I fell into this category. . . . In those days, it was extremely difficult for anyone born in Asia, as we were, to immigrate to America. So this new quota was great news to us—a door into America—the land of liberty and opportunity, the land of an immigrant's dreams."

The Land of Opportunity

In 1961, Joyce arrived in California alone. "My mother stayed in Holland so that if I could not make it in America, I could return there. . . . America exceeded my wildest expectations. All I had expected was an assembly-line job in a factory. Instead, 'fresh off the boat,' so to speak, I was hired as a secretary at a large insurance company with a salary of $280 a month."

"Today I can truly say that I have lived the impossible dream. My success could have happened only in America."

Six years later, Joyce was able to realize her dream of getting a college education. "My mother passed away and left me her entire life savings of five thousand dollars. I know she had scraped that together for me at great personal sacrifice. . . . I became a college freshman at the age of twenty-seven and completed four years of college coursework in three years, while still working at least twenty hours a week to help pay my expenses." Despite this difficult schedule, Joyce graduated from the University of California *magna cum laude* and Phi Beta Kappa.

Her boss encouraged her to make the transition from working for him as a legal secretary to becoming a lawyer in her own right. Taking the challenge, Joyce pursued a joint degree program in law and public administration at the University of Southern California; her masters' thesis earned the school's "Outstanding Thesis" award.

She gained experience as an attorney for a dozen years, first in the State Attorney General's Office and then as a research attorney in the State Court of Appeal. In the mid-eighties, Governor George Deukmejian appointed her to be a judge on the Municipal Court. He then advanced her over each of the next three years with appointments to the state's Superior Court, Court of Appeal, and Supreme Court. She has been on the California Supreme Court since 1989—only the second woman to serve on the seven-member court.

Joyce has earned a reputation as an independent thinker who does not shirk from disagreeing with her colleagues. She has put her name to numerous dissenting opinions to prove it. Before she was appointed, some people thought she would fit a certain "moderate conservative" role, and she must have disappointed them—and perhaps pleased others—when she did not play out their expectations.

For example, one case in which she may have surprised people is a lead opinion she wrote for a case where the California Supreme Court prohibited school-endorsed prayers in public school graduation ceremonies. The Court advanced the public policy that in a religiously diverse society, religious neutrality must be respected.[1] In the opinion, Joyce wrote, "Respect for the differing religious choices of the people of this country requires that government neither place its stamp of approval on any particular religious practice, nor appear to take a stand on any religious question. In a world frequently torn by religious factionalism and the violence tragically associated with political division along religious lines, our nation's position of governmental neutrality on religious matters stands as an illuminating example of the true meaning of freedom and tolerance."

Only in America

Today Joyce is in a position where she impacts many people's lives. She asserts, "While I was growing up on the Indonesian island of Java, later in the jungles of New Guinea, and then as a teenager in Holland, I never imagined in my wildest dreams that one day I would be lucky enough to live in the United States. I never thought that I would ever be an attorney. I never thought that I would ever be a judge. Today I can truly say that I have lived the impossible dream. My success could have happened only in America.

"I have a deep love for America. America gave me a chance to get an education when I was well beyond normal school age. America gave me a chance to succeed against all odds. And America taught me that the boundaries of achievement are set largely by the individual. As former President Lyndon Johnson said, 'America is the uncrossed desert and the unclimbed

[1] *Sands v. Morong Unified School District,* 53 Cal. 863, 884 (1991).

ridge.' There's so much to be gained by setting out to conquer those yet unclimbed ridges."

Joyce has other advice to share. "Have integrity. Temper your drive for success by fair play and fair dealing, which is a concept that has withstood the test of time. . . . The ethical dimensions of life are not incompatible with success. To the contrary! It is only by adhering to the highest standards of ethics and fair play that one can become truly successful and respected. Finally, don't give up on ideals, on dreams. In the words of the poet Langston Hughes, 'Hold fast to dreams, for if dreams die, life is a broken-winged bird that cannot fly.'"

Joyce Kennard followed a curving path to pursue her education and profession and then steered onto a relatively straightforward career course. Pat Wald obtained her education via a direct route and then put aside career to raise a family, later re-entering and advancing in her profession by less direct means. These two complementary tales illustrate the advantage of continuing with education, career, and self-improvement in the midst of—or in spite of—more pressing life situations, and the value of applying long-term perspective to such efforts.

> *"Have integrity. Temper your drive for success by fair play and fair dealing, which is a concept that has withstood the test of time. . . . It is only by adhering to the highest standards of ethics and fair play that one can become truly successful and respected."*

XIII.

ANTONIA
HERNANDEZ

Spending time with Antonia Hernandez made me think about my teachers.

The first grown-up who wasn't related to me who reached out to start a friendship was Mrs. Geruson, my high school English teacher. I was fourteen years old. She was something between a parent and a friend. The great thing about her was she knew a lot more about a lot of things than my other friends, yet her advice was more fun and hip than listening to my mother.

One day her son, a college student, visited our class. He talked about "college life." I remember he was wearing (and I'm not one to remember what people are wearing) a "fisherman's sweater"—off-white, crew neck, long rows of rope stitching, hanging to his hips—with faded blue jeans and white leather sneakers. And I remember looking at him and thinking, "So that's what a college student looks like."

He told us he had changed his high school study habits and become more self-disciplined because college had fewer day-to-day assignments, more projects and term papers. He explained how he lived within a budget and the expenses of being a college student. He told us he had recently started dating a girl who, when he first asked her out, said, "If you didn't ask me out soon, I was just going to ask you out!" He said he would not have minded if she had asked him out first (and I filed that away as an important thing to know about college boys). Once I made it to college, I can't tell you how many times I remembered things from his conversation with our class that day.

After high school, I stayed friends with Mrs. Geruson. I also got to know her son and her husband. In college, I even became the proud owner of a fisherman's sweater. When I wore my "college student outfit"—which was that sweater with jeans and sneakers—I knew I would be fitting in just fine anywhere around campus.

Mrs. Geruson remained available for advice. My girlfriends and I went to visit her at home for dessert and to talk about college life. She was thrilled when I was admitted to NYU Law School. I remember sitting in my bedroom on the phone with her, the two of us just screaming in delight and celebration. Then when I was a few years out of school, she passed away. I was told she had been sick in the hospital for a few weeks first; if I had known, I would have dropped everything to go and visit her.

I moved back to Philadelphia a few years after that. One day I happened to be in the building where I knew Mrs. Geruson's son worked, so I stopped by. When he walked out to say hello, I saw her face so clearly in his face, and I started to cry. We hugged and cried together.

The conversations in this book are like the conversations I used to have with Mrs. Geruson, like the one her son had with our class that day. They can really make a difference to the person who is there to listen and learn— they are not forgotten; they are drawn from again and again. They are savored and become sweeter with time.

Although there are plenty of differences between myself and Antonia Hernandez, I bonded with her because of something we both have had that is exactly the same: a group of grown-ups who really wanted the best for us and really wanted to help.

Antonia Hernandez walks through the elegant wood-paneled corridors of the Mexican American Legal Defense and Educational Fund ("MALDEF") in the art deco-era Banks Huntley Building in downtown Los Angeles, explaining some recent endeavors for MALDEF. MALDEF is this country's chief advocacy group for Latino rights, and Antonia is MALDEF's president and general counsel. As she enters her impressive office, and settles in behind her desk, the questions in the air are, "How did she get

---

Antonia Hernandez

RESIDENCE: Los Angeles, California
BORN: 1948
PROFESSIONAL: President and General Counsel, Mexican American Legal Defense and Educational Fund
PERSONAL: Married (2 children)
1997 Recipient of the Margaret Brent Award

---

here, and how could someone else get here?" Antonia goes on to share the story of how the support of family and others—combined with her own drive to succeed—brought her from a ranch in Mexico to where she sits today.

"I had a very happy childhood," Antonia begins. "I grew up in the 1950s as a poor girl, but unaware of things other people had that I didn't have. My family lived on an *ejido* [a communal ranch] in Mexico with several hundred other people—many of whom were related to us."

Antonia's family moved to California when she was eight. They lived in an East Los Angeles housing project. She remembers, "My mother used to make us sweep the sidewalk in front of the project. And she would give us Comet cleanser to scrub graffiti off the exterior walls. My mom really believed cleanliness was next to godliness. . . . Used *National Geographic* magazines were always in our house. Although my parents did not read English, the magazines had symbolic value—they meant that we valued increasing our knowledge of the big wide world."

During the summer, the seven children in the family contributed to the household by picking crops with their parents in the San Joaquin Valley. Antonia recollects, "It was hard labor. The four oldest of us were girls. My parents never told me and my sisters that we couldn't do something because we were girls. They needed us to work hard for the family. My sisters and I grew up never shying away from anything.

"When I think back, I can't believe how little my parents had, and yet how much they gave us. My parents' message was simple and never-changing. Sometimes they said it, and sometimes you felt it: 'Work hard at everything you do. . . . Be proud of who you are. . . . You're all that matters to us. We'll make sacrifices for you so that you can be educated and have a better life.'"

The Importance of Teachers

Reflecting upon the role teachers played in her development, Antonia describes how one of her grade-school teachers would ask her to stay after school to assist with organizing the classroom. "She told me she asked me to help her because of how smart I was. That made me want to be smarter. . . . A teacher's perception of a student can help shape that student's development—call it self-fulfilling prophecy. . . . When a student is treated as incompetent, you encourage their incompetence. When a student is treated as competent, you encourage the development of their confidence in their abilities. . . . If you know your teacher thinks you're a smart girl, and you're confronted with a new situation, you'll think, 'How does a smart girl act in this situation?' and that's the way you'll act, striving for smart choices."

Antonia also encountered teachers of the discouraging variety. One of her high school teachers gave a writing assignment on the topic, "What I want to be when I grow up." She wrote an essay about how she wanted to go to college when she grew up. The reaction of Antonia's teacher was very discouraging—and almost unbelievable knowing all that she's since achieved. "He drew a sad face on top of my essay. . . . He wrote next to the sad face, 'Not college material—start thinking about other options.' I couldn't believe a teacher told me I wasn't 'college material' when I was an A-student. What was 'college material' then? I don't know why he discouraged me—my gender? My ethnicity? My lack of intelligence?

"I have since learned that people can harbor beliefs and assumptions that lead to prejudice even when they mean well. . . . It may just be easiest to like and to promote those who most remind us of ourselves. . . . Fortunately, this teacher's mixed message—rejecting my goal without good reason, but couched in a supportive way—did not hurt me. I was mature enough and had received enough positive feedback from my parents and from other teachers to know I was on a course headed for college. Yet his comments still deflated me."

After high school, Antonia attended the college nearest to home—East Los Angeles Junior College. She joined the school's Mexican American Student Association and participated regularly in student protests. Her parents remained protective and supportive: "I remember sitting in the kitchen one night explaining to my father why it was so important for me to participate in a protest against the Safeway supermarket for selling grapes picked by Mexican migrant workers. When I convinced my dad this was a worthwhile and safe activity for me, we chose a nearby landmark for him to drop me off and pick me up from the protest."

"If you know your teacher thinks you're a smart girl, and you're confronted with a new situation, you'll think, 'How does a smart girl act in this situation?' and that's the way you'll act, striving for smart choices."

In college, Antonia met the teacher who did the most to advance her development. She sighs with a smile, "Dr. Helen Bailey, the chair of the History Department of East L.A. College, was the most fascinating person I ever met. . . . She dressed bohemian. . . . She had traveled to China and Tahiti. . . . I wanted to be educated like her. She advised me to expand my course of study by going to the University of California at Los Angeles ("UCLA"). . . . It was on the other side of town, but I didn't even know it existed. It was part of the Anglo world, of which I knew very little. . . . With her encouragement, I applied to UCLA."

A Whole New World

Before she could transfer schools, though, Antonia would have to address her parents' reaction to the news that she had been accepted to UCLA. "I knew the sensitive part would be that it was a far commute, so I would have to live there. For all that my parents gave me free rein when something involved work for the family or for school, I knew in one respect they were extremely traditional: no one in our family left their parents' home until they married. I told my mom Dr. Bailey believed it was the best thing for me professionally. I knew my mother trusted my teachers and would never want to stand in the way. . . . She knew how hard I worked at my schoolwork. . . . As I waited for her reaction, I was so scared she would reject the idea and crush my hopes. Eyeball-to-eyeball, she said to me, 'We're going to have to work on your dad.'"

Antonia's father eventually consented to the transfer, and she began preparing to enter the "Anglo world" of UCLA. Money was put aside for new school clothes. She recounts, "My mother and I went shopping for a suitcase and then filled it with new clothes from Lerner's. . . . The day before the first day of school, my whole family drove me to UCLA in our big beige car—Mom, Dad, six kids, and that suitcase. Before my family left, my father walked all through the dormitory to make sure no boys lived there and to check the security system."

Antonia befriended her roommate, the first Anglo person with whom she had ever spent time outside of school. She elaborates, "My roommate had blonde hair and blue eyes. She wanted to be a historian. She was serious about her schoolwork and was a very positive influence on me."

This time of change and assimilation is remembered fondly. "For me, the process of 'becoming American' was first perfecting the language, then learning the styles, and finally making friends who had been born here. My family retained many Mexican traditions and customs we brought with us, while striving to take advantage of the opportunities this country offered. . . . I had a fire in my belly during those years. I remember feeling it in the morning while I dressed—that I wanted to get out there and accomplish things. I hadn't been integrated enough into the real world yet to know the obstacles that were waiting for me, based upon being a minority twice—as a female and a person of color. Failure was not an option I ever thought about. Looking back, I can see the positive side of that, because when you take the time to very clearly lay out all your limitations, they truly *become* your limitations."

A UCLA professor of history told Antonia he thought she would make a good lawyer, but Antonia had planned to teach after graduation. Her family was expecting her to contribute some of her income to help her sisters and brothers to attend college. Attending law school would mean postponing the earning of income for three more years. But her teacher's advice persuaded her to yet again take the path her parents never expected. "Dr. Bradford knew I wanted to help Latinas, and he told me the law was the best vehicle for change. He challenged me that if I really wanted to help my people, the law was the way to do it.

"I had a fire in my belly during those years. . . . Failure was not an option I ever thought about. Looking back, I can see the positive side of that, because when you take the time to very clearly lay out all your limitations, they truly become your limitations."

"So at home, it was the same procedure again as with the transfer to UCLA. . . . I told my mom about my desire to attend law school before I told my dad. I told her I had the support of my teacher, and she told me, 'We'll work on your dad.' I decided to broach the topic with my father that night. My uncle was visiting. Their first reactions to my going to law school are still vivid. . . . My father said, 'Why do you want to be a lawyer? They're a bunch of thieves.' My uncle said, 'You can't be a lawyer. You're a girl.' . . . My father was predictable, though. After I explained why this would make me happy, he said he would support me."

Career on the Rise

Antonia graduated from UCLA Law School in 1974 and worked as a staff attorney with the Los Angeles Center for Law and Justice and then the Legal Aid Foundation of Los Angeles. In 1979, she was hired as counsel to the United States Senate Judiciary Committee, then chaired by Senator Ted Kennedy (D-Massachusetts), and moved to Washington, D.C. Her family was honored to have her serve Senator Kennedy. Antonia comments, "The Kennedy family was revered by Mexican-Americans for their record of supporting Mexican-Americans on issues important to us. Robert F. Kennedy is especially remembered for his civil rights work. . . . John F. Kennedy was the first Catholic President, and Ethel Kennedy even visited Cesar Chavez when he was imprisoned for trying to unionize the grape-pickers in California. . . . Mexican-Americans from all over the country write to Senator Kennedy with their concerns.

"On my first day, Senator Kennedy called a meeting to welcome the new staff members. He said, 'Always be fair, but always pursue what we want. . . . Represent me well.' The one thing about Senator Kennedy I never stopped appreciating was the direct access he provided to himself. That is a leadership skill I have tried to emulate. Anytime I needed feedback on anything, I just wrote it up in a memo and put it in a pouch kept on his desk. The black bag was sent to wherever the Senator was, and you always had his feedback or approval by phone or by memo within forty-eight hours."

> *"The one thing about Senator Kennedy I never stopped appreciating was the direct access he provided to himself. That is a leadership skill I have tried to emulate."*

When Republicans took control of the Senate in 1981, most of the Kennedy staff had to find new jobs, including Antonia. She became the director of MALDEF's Washington, D.C., office. Since 1985, she has been MALDEF's president and general counsel, working to promote and to protect the civil rights of the tens of millions of American-Latinos in education, employment, immigration, and voting access. MALDEF also has brought many of the lawsuits resulting in greater Hispanic political representation.

She states, "I get paid to do what I love to do. If you can find a job you love to do and it helps humanity, you'll be blessed as I have been. . . . But no matter where you are in life or how you make a living, I suggest seeking variety in your life experiences—and getting to know people of color and the poor."

Antonia leans back in her chair and looks upward, seemingly looking back over the tale of her journey she has shared. "I am the product of the good will of good people who saw something in me and gave me opportunities. I am where I am thanks to Mom and Dad, my brothers and sisters, my teachers, mentors, and colleagues. . . . Each time somebody provided me with a new opportunity, I did my best to produce for them and make them not regret that they had given me the chance to prove myself. And I try to use the position I have as a result of all their good will to do good for others."

"I get paid to do what I love to do. If you can find a job you love to do and it helps humanity, you'll be blessed as I have been."

XIV.
RUTH BADER
GINSBURG

In the days leading up to my meeting with Justice Ruth Bader Ginsburg of the United States Supreme Court, a piece of striking news footage came to mind repeatedly: It was Ruth Ginsburg, standing in the Rose Garden of the White House in 1993, as she accepted President Clinton's Supreme Court nomination. She evoked the memory of her mother—"the bravest and strongest person I have ever known, who was taken from me much too soon. I pray that I may be all that she would have been, had she lived in an age when women could aspire and achieve and daughters are cherished as much as sons." President Clinton, standing nearby, was moved to tears.

The poignancy of the new justice's image stemmed from the fact that we truly live not only in a new age, but in a new world, for women—one that female ancestors might not recognize, much as they might have dreamed of it.

Ginsburg's words made me think about my mother's life, my grandmother's life, and everything they did to encourage me in pursuing a career. I thought about how their lives would be different if they were girls growing up in America today.

While I was in grade school, my grandmother (who lived with us) was in charge every afternoon until my mom got home from school or work. Grandmom, an immigrant who spoke broken English, had not received much formal education. She was absolutely in awe of school and what it could do for a person. My grandmother's pride in clearing off the kitchen table from 3:00 to 5:00 P.M. so I could spread out my homework was palpable. I knew how pleased she was that I was an A-student who wanted to be a lawyer. I know she would be proud of me today.

There is no doubt that Justice Ginsburg has lived up to her mother's greatest hopes for her—after all, she has done no less than to alter the social and legal status of American women.

Justice Ginsburg is relaxing in a quiet reception room at Atlanta's Ritz-Carlton Hotel, where she will accept the American Bar Association's Thurgood Marshall Award later in the evening. When I explained to her that I've never forgotten her eloquent tribute to her mother in the Rose Garden when she was sworn in, she explains, "My mother influenced my life more than anyone else. She was extremely intelligent, a prolific reader, caring, and resourceful. . . . She completed high school at fifteen,

Ruth Bader Ginsburg

RESIDENCE: Washington, D.C.
HOMETOWN: Brooklyn, New York
BORN: 1933
PERSONAL: Married (two children)
PROFESSIONAL: Associate Justice, Supreme Court of the United States
1993 Recipient of the Margaret Brent Award

always earning top grades. She got a job and contributed part of her income to support her older brother in college. She never attended college, despite what her dreams for herself may have been. From a young age, I knew she was putting aside part of her 'pin money' for me to go to college. . . . She passed away the day before my high school graduation. It is a comfort she knew I was going to start Cornell University in the fall—the school her brother had attended." The description Ruth provides of her mother is a reminder that even though women in the past were not always in the forefront of the political or business scene, they have long influenced others to achieve their very best.

At Cornell, Ruth met Martin Ginsburg, who was a year ahead of her. They decided to pursue careers in law together. After his graduation, Martin began studying at Harvard Law School. They married shortly after Ruth's graduation from Cornell. Before they could study law together, however, they moved to Fort Sill, Oklahoma, for two years—during which time Martin was in the service and their daughter Jane was born. In 1956, Ruth began her law studies at Harvard and Martin resumed his. When Martin graduated and accepted a position in New York City, Ruth transferred to Columbia Law School for her last year of study. She graduated from Columbia in 1959, tied for first in her class. Because she had completed two years of study at Harvard, Ruth was later offered a Harvard Law School degree, contingent upon her returning her degree from Columbia. She refused to do so.

Ginsburg & Ginsburg

Graduating ranked first in the class from an Ivy League law school such as Columbia can be a stepping stone to a Supreme Court clerkship and job offers from prestigious law firms. In 1959, however, this stepping stone could only be tread upon by males. One of Ruth's professors at Harvard recommended her highly for a Supreme Court clerkship, but reported back to her that Justice Felix Frankfurter had said he "wasn't ready to hire a woman." No prestigious law firms came knocking. "Firms were just starting to turn around on hiring Jews. Here I was, a woman, a Jew, and a mother—it was a bit much for them!" After a lower court federal clerkship and authoring a book on Swedish civil procedure, Ruth began teaching at Rutgers Law School and volunteered to litigate cases with the American Civil Liberties Union ("ACLU"). She later held teaching positions at Columbia and Harvard law schools.

"Firms were just starting to turn around on hiring Jews. Here I was, a woman, a Jew, and a mother—it was a bit much for them!"

"Fortunately, in my marriage I didn't get second-class treatment," she smiles. "My marriage provided an environment of equality, in which I felt respected and cherished. It was a source of strength. . . . Whenever I needed to travel for work, Martin happily took over the primary caretaker role—something few men did at the time. When he tasted my tuna casserole, could not tell what it was, and asked whether I had cooked dinosaur, he decided he would simply take over cooking for the family. He had fun with it—he told me he thought of cooking as mixing things in a chemistry lab and became a really great cook.

"My unconventional husband encouraged my growing interest in women's place in the world and questions of gender equality. And so it was appropriate that my first foray into women and the law was a team effort with him. . . . In 1970, he was flipping through summaries of tax rulings at home and dropped one in my lap, saying, 'You'll find this interesting.' He was right. I found it fascinating.

"A traveling salesman, named Charles Moritz, claimed a dependent care deduction on his taxes for money spent to take care of his eighty-nine-year-old mother while he traveled for business. The Internal Revenue Service ("IRS") disallowed the deduction and ruled it was only for women—or men who were married, divorced, or widowed. Mr. Moritz was single, so the IRS said he could not claim this deduction. Moritz argued *pro se* [he represented himself, with no attorney] before the tax court that he would have been allowed the deduction if he were a dutiful daughter instead of a dutiful son. I read the summary and said, 'Let's take this case!' So my husband called Charles Moritz, and we prepared an appeal brief for him.[1] I provided constitutional law analysis and Marty provided tax analysis. The remedy we sought from the court was not to invalidate the statute, but to apply it equally to both sexes." The Ginsburg team's arguments prevailed. The appeals court reversed the lower court decision and held that the taxpayer (Mr. Moritz) was entitled to the dependent care deduction. Ruth comments, "My husband calls that brief the 'grandmother brief' because it was the first time I thought through the legal analysis for a gender discrimination issue. He jokes that everything I did after that was really just recycling the same brief over and over again. He's not entirely wrong."

Using the Law to Fight Inequality

Soon after her work on the *Moritz* case, Ruth would take that gender discrimination analysis all the way to the United States Supreme Court. She

[1] *Moritz v. Commissioner,* 55 T.C. 113, 115 (1970), *rev'd* 469 F.2d 466 (10th Cir. 1972), *cert denied* 412 U.S. 906 (1973).

remembers, "The director of the ACLU's national office asked me to work with him on a case the Supreme Court had just accepted for review. The case was very simple: Sally Reed's teenage son died under tragic circumstances, and she applied to be administrator of his estate. The boy's father—the parents were separated—also applied to be administrator. The state of Idaho had a rule for deciding such cases. The rule was that between persons equally entitled to administer a decedent's estate, males must be preferred to females.[2] . . . I am sure it's astonishing to younger people that laws like that were on the books in the United States in the early 1970s, but they were— and there were many more.

"We urged the Supreme Court to recognize the equal stature of men and women. The Supreme Court had interpreted the Fourteenth Amendment's Equal Protection Clause[3] as prohibiting discrimination based on race and requiring 'strict scrutiny' of any law drawing a race-based distinction. I believed any sex-based distinction warranted the same scrutiny." The Supreme Court found the law at issue in Reed to be unconstitutional. For the first time in the 103-year history of the Fourteenth Amendment, the Supreme Court ruled that the Equal Protection Clause protected women's rights. Following the success in Reed, the ACLU established a Women's Rights Project with Ginsburg as codirector.

But Women Are Treated Better than Men . . .

Ruth saw her role both as an advocate and as a teacher. She explains, "The enormous difference between fighting gender discrimination as opposed to race discrimination is good people immediately perceive race discrimination as evil and intolerable. But when I talked about sex-based discrimination, I got the response, 'What are you talking about? Women are treated ever so much better than men!' They took what I said as criticism of the way they treated their

---

[2] *Reed v. Reed,* 404 U.S. 71 (1971).

[3] The Fourteenth Amendment to the U.S. Constitution provides, "No state shall make or enforce any law which shall abridge the privileges or immunities of citizens of the United States; nor shall any state deprive any person of life, liberty, or property without due process of law; nor deny to any person within its jurisdiction the equal protection of the laws."

wives, mothers, and daughters. Judges needed to be educated that old notions were limiting the opportunities and aspirations of women in this country.

Justice Ginsburg shares the story of Gwendolyn Hoyt to demonstrate women's place under the law before she applied her considerable talents to changing women's place: "A good example of the starting point from which this process began is a Supreme Court case from the early sixties on whether women should be required to serve on juries or whether, as Florida had it, women who wanted to serve on juries had to sign up in the court's office—with the result that very few did.[4] . . . The facts of the underlying case were these: Gwendolyn Hoyt had a philandering husband who regularly humiliated her to the breaking point. We didn't have terms like 'battered woman' in those days, but she did not have a happy marriage. One day, in a rage at the humiliation to which she was exposed, she turned to the corner of the room and spied an old broken baseball bat. She brought it down on the head of her husband—ending the fight, ending his life, and starting a murder prosecution.

"Gwendolyn was convicted of murder by an all-male jury. . . . Her

> *"The enormous difference between fighting gender discrimination as opposed to race discrimination is good people immediately perceive race discrimination as evil and intolerable. But when I talked about sex-based discrimination, I got the response, 'What are you talking about? Women are treated ever so much better than men!'"*

argument to the Supreme Court was that women on the jury—or at least in the pool from which the jury was picked—would better understand her state

[4] *Hoyt v. Florida*, 368 U.S. 57, 61–64 (1961).

of mind, her utter frustration, and would improve her chances of being convicted of something less than murder. . . . The Court found that Gwendolyn
Hoyt's not being given a jury pool drawn from a fair cross section of men and
women is purely a favor to women. Women have the best of both worlds—
they can serve if they want to, and they don't have to serve if they don't want

> *"The law had been contributing to the perpetuation of gender stereotypes. We now had to use the law to abolish these iniquities."*

to. In essence, they responded to her
plea by saying that women are treated
better than men, so there is nothing to
complain about. . . . No one riveted
attention on her underlying murder
conviction, which was left standing."
Ruth continues, "The law had been
contributing to the perpetuation of
gender stereotypes. We now had to use
the law to abolish these iniquities."

Women Can Be Independent

Ginsburg then executed a strategy to accomplish this goal: Cases would be
chosen for sequential presentations before the Supreme Court to attack the
most pervasive stereotype in the law at the time—that men are independent
and women are men's dependents.

She describes how the use of a male plaintiff assisted in making a clear,
easy-to-understand case of how gender stereotyping harms both men and
women: "We had a male client, Stephen Wiesenfeld, who—like Sally Reed—
had suffered a tragedy. His wife died while giving birth to their first child. He
was given a healthy baby son, and he decided to stay home and raise his child.
When he went to the local Social Security office and asked about the benefits
a sole surviving parent could get, he was told that benefit is called a 'mother's
benefit' and he didn't qualify. . . . He wrote a letter to the editor of the local
newspaper. He started his letter, 'I've heard a lot about women's lib. Let me tell
you my story.' He explained how his wife had been a wage-earner, paid the
same Social Security tax a man would pay, yet he didn't qualify as a care-giv-

ing parent who could collect her child protective death benefit because he was male. His letter ended, 'Tell *that* to Gloria Steinem!'"

The Supreme Court rendered a unanimous judgment in favor of Stephen Wiesenfeld's right to collect his wife's death benefit, striking down the gender-based classification.[5] "Wiesenfeld's case shows the irrationality of gender-based classifications," Justice Ginsburg observes. "Consider his wife—she worked as a man did, paid the same Social Security tax as a male wage-earner, but the government would not protect her family the way it protected the family of a male wage-earner. . . . Then there was the husband, Stephen—he wanted to care for his child, but was told there were no benefits to do that because he was a male parent, not a female parent. . . . And there was the baby, Jason: he could not have the opportunity to have the care of his surviving parent, for the sole reason that it was his mother who died instead of his father."

An Impressive Record

Through the seventies, Ginsburg argued six and won five of the first and most important cases regarding equal rights for women and men before the Supreme Court—an amazing record of Supreme Court advocacy.[6] In addition, the Court accepted Ruth's view that challenges to gender-based discrimination deserve heightened scrutiny in *Craig v. Boren*, 429 U.S. 190 (1976) (in which Ruth filed a "friend of the court" brief). Kathleen Peratis, a former codirector of the ACLU Women's Law Project, described what it was like to work with Ruth on gender discrimination cases. "She wasn't just a wonderful lawyer. She was a visionary. . . . When we worked together at the ACLU, I knew Ruth would someday be on the Supreme Court—and we hoped become chief justice. . . . Step-by-step she made things happen that women

---

[5] *Weinberger v. Wiesenfeld*, 420 U.S. 636 (1975).

[6] The six Supreme Court cases Ruth argued, using the Fourteenth Amendment to erase gender discrimination, are: *Frontiero v. Richardson*, 411 U.S. 677 (1973); *Kahn v. Shevin*, 416 U.S. 351 (1974); *Edwards v. Healy*, 421 U.S. 772 (1975); *Weinberger v. Wiesenfeld*, 420 U.S. 636 (1975); *Califano v. Goldfarb*, 430 U.S. 199 (1977); and *Duren v. Missouri*, 439 U.S. 357 (1979).

had been dreaming about for a hundred years. Ruth's work for women is transcendent in the history of this country."

Two presidents confirmed Kathleen's assessment. In 1980, President Carter appointed Ginsburg to the United States Court of Appeals for the D.C. Circuit. In 1993, President Clinton, impressed by her sparkling record on the appellate court and by the significant precedents for women's rights she had set, hailed her as "the Thurgood Marshall of gender-equality law"—and elevated her to the Supreme Court.

Conquering Male Strongholds

In 1996, the Supreme Court decided that the exclusion of women from the Virginia Military Institute ("VMI") violated the Equal Protection Clause of the Fourteenth Amendment. Thus, the Commonwealth of Virginia could not exclude women from attending a public military college (VMI) if they met the entrance requirements. Fittingly, Justice Ginsburg wrote the Court's opinion, noting, "'inherent differences' between men and women, we have come to appreciate, remain cause for celebration, but not for denigration of the members of either sex or for artificial constraints on an individual's opportunity. . . . [S]uch classifications may not be used, as they once were, to create or perpetuate the legal, social, and economic inferiority of women."[7]

Ginsburg tells of a touching letter she received after the VMI decision: "A 1967 graduate of VMI wrote to say he knows a few young women today who are physically, intellectually, and emotionally tougher than he was when he first attended! He said since he made it through, he knew they would make it, too. . . . He wrote again a few months later and enclosed a pin given to the mothers of the graduating cadets at his graduation. His mother is now deceased, and his family decided they wanted me to have her pin—as an adjunct member of the 'VMI family.' . . . In his words, as a 'mother' to VMI's first and succeeding women graduates. . . . It is a gift I treasure."

And "like mother, like daughter" (as the saying will have to become),

[7] *United States v. Virginia*, 116 S. Ct. 2264, 2275-76 (1996).

Ruth's daughter Jane has also pursued a profession in law. Ruth speaks of Jane Ginsburg with pride and affection. Jane is an authority on copyright law who teaches at Columbia Law School. They share a love of the law. "We are the first mother-daughter pair to have attended Harvard Law School," Ruth reports, "and the first pair to serve on a law faculty in the United States (Columbia). . . . Consider this—yet another example of how the world has changed since I started on my way. At Harvard Law School in 1956, I was one of nine women in a class of over five hundred. By the time Jane attended in the late seventies, her class had one hundred women. Today there are at least twice that number in every starting class. . . . While I was there, I never imagined females would infiltrate a male bastion like Harvard Law School in those numbers."

The Supreme Court must still be regarded a male bastion, as Ginsburg—the 107th Supreme Court Justice in this country's history—is only the second female to serve. She states, "I am glad to contribute to the end of the days when women, at least half the talent pool in our society, appear in high places as one-at-a-time performers."

" . . . 'Inherent differences' between men and women, we have come to appreciate, remain cause for celebration, but not for denigration of the members of either sex or for artificial constraints on an individual's opportunity. . . . [S]uch classifications may not be used, as they once were, to create or perpetuate the legal, social, and economic inferiority of women."

Sisterhood among the Brethren

Of the first woman appointed to the Court, Justice Sandra Day O'Connor, Ginsburg comments, "Justice O'Connor also met with gender discrimination when she entered the work world. She graduated from Stanford Law School in 1952 at the top of her class. Our Chief Justice, William Rehnquist, was in her class. He also ranked at the top. Rehnquist got a Supreme Court clerkship, a much sought-after job for young lawyers. Not only was that opportunity not available to Sandra Day, but no firm would hire her to do a lawyer's work. She was offered jobs only as a legal secretary.

"I am glad to contribute to the end of the days when women, at least half the talent pool in our society, appear in high places as one-at-a-time performers."

"When I first arrived at the Court, Justice O'Connor was like a big sister—telling me many things to make my life easier. We may be on opposite sides in cases, but we respect each other. . . . For instance, there is a myth that the first opinion assigned to a new justice is a unanimous, easy case. My first assignment was not so easy, and the decision was six to three. Justice O'Connor joined the dissent. As I read a summary of my opinion from the bench, I was passed a note by a messenger. The note said: 'This is your first opinion for the Court. It is a fine opinion. I look forward to many more.' The note was signed 'Sandra.'"

The Thurgood Marshall Award

The American Bar Association's Thurgood Marshall Award recognizes long-term contributions to the advancement of civil rights in the United States. Thurgood Marshall himself received the inaugural award in 1992. When Ginsburg accepted the award a few hours after our conversation, she invoked its namesake—the person with whom she is most often compared—Thurgood Marshall:

My chambers, some of you may know, are the only Justice's quarters upstairs at the Supreme Court. The rooms were Justice Marshall's from the time of his retirement until his death. Now and again I am invited to move downstairs, but I am glad to stay in my current space. Across the room where I work, on a bookshelf I can see from my desk, there is a photograph of Justice Marshall, Ninth Circuit Judge Clifford Wallace, and me. . . .

Marshall's advice to his law clerks was in tune with his signal achievement, his careful orchestration of the campaign that culminated after many preparatory years in *Brown v. Board of Education*. He told his clerks that, to avoid exhaustion and burnout, one must carefully choose the battles one will fight. . . .

My advocacy, of course, did not begin to compare with Thurgood Marshall's. My life was never in danger, and the ACLU litigation I superintended was never the only show in town. Unlike the 1940s' and 1950s' efforts to achieve racial justice, controlled by Thurgood Marshall and his colleagues, sex discrimination litigation, from the start, was dispersed, with many, often uncoordinated, players on the scene. But of one thing there is no doubt. I gained courage and inspiration from Marshall's example—his measured step-by-step strategy; his understanding that it was necessary to educate his audience; his provision of that education in ways comprehensible by, and palatable to, the decision-makers.

When Ginsburg stops speaking, a long-lasting applause begins and swells. She remains at the podium and smiles. Her demeanor is modest, gracious. And it is evident that the audience needs to give this outpouring of appreciation and admiration to her much more than she needs to receive it. She has been accustomed to working for so many years in silence, without accolades or recognition. Ruth Bader Ginsburg's work as an advocate, an educator, and a spokesperson has provided women opportunities in a new landscape—to achieve and aspire, to tread upon stepping stones, to climb ridges, and to reach for the stars.

XV.
NORMA
SHAPIRO

Norma Shapiro and I worked about ten blocks from each other in downtown Philadelphia.

I left my office to walk to our meeting and headed toward City Hall—with its statue of William Penn shimmering atop it in the morning sun. Penn founded Philadelphia in 1682. Choosing the name because it means "City of Brother-*ly Love," it comported with his goal of establishing a city on the precepts of religious freedom and civil liberty. I wondered what he would think of the changing roles of women in his city.*

Then I walked through City Hall and down Market Street toward Independence Hall. There, almost a century after the founding of Philadelphia, a committee comprised of the brightest minds in the Continental Congress—Benjamin Franklin of Philadelphia, John Adams of Massachusetts, and Thomas Jefferson of Virginia—met to draw up the reasons why America should declare its independence from England. This resulted in Jefferson's drafting of the Declaration of Independence, with its assertion "All men *are created equal." Likewise, as I walked, I mulled over what the Founding Fathers might have to say about all the women I had been meeting and their efforts on behalf of other women.*

Across the street from Independence Hall is the federal courthouse. I entered and looked for Norma, the last "counselor" with whom I would be meeting. By this time I was on part-time status at my law firm, to give me the time to pull together the interviews and produce a manuscript.

And by this time, I had started to think about the path I would take after I made this manuscript as good as I possibly could and left the law firm. All I knew for sure was that, anymore, I didn't think anything was worth dedicating myself to unless I felt it could help those who come behind us and make the world better for them. I decided Penn, Franklin, Adams, and Jefferson would agree with me. That's what they were all about. And I decided the counselors I had met so far would agree with me, as that's what they're all about too.

I would have to put my mind to this and figure it out for myself very soon. For the moment, with a little tug of sadness at my heart, I walked into Norma's chambers for the last of the conversations.

The hallways leading to Norma Shapiro's judicial chambers in the federal courthouse are lined with annual group photographs of the judges who have served there. None of these photos includes a woman's face in the sea of distinguished-looking gentlemen until 1978. Until Norma Shapiro. Norma Shapiro is the first female to be appointed to the federal bench in the Third Circuit, which encompasses the federal courts of Pennsylvania, New Jersey, Delaware, and the Virgin Islands.

Norma Shapiro

RESIDENCE: Philadelphia, Pennsylvania
BORN: 1928
PERSONAL: Married (3 children)
POSITION: U.S. District Court Judge, Eastern District of Pennsylvania
1999 Recipient of the Margaret Brent Award

Seated at the conference table in her chambers, Norma comments on the composition of the photos in the outer hallway. "I certainly was lonely for a time," she says, mildly, but emphatically. "For years I had no one with whom to share feminine insights. I felt left out of informal meetings and socializing among the judges, and I was the only woman at our formal gatherings and meetings. There was hardly ever a woman in the halls. It was sometimes a difficult atmosphere."

It was necessary to become accustomed to being the only woman in the room, however. When she practiced law before becoming a judge, Norma was the first woman admitted to partnership at her firm—one of the largest in the city. In fact, she was one of the first few women to make partner in any of Philadelphia's major law firms. She was the first woman to serve on, and the first woman to chair, the Philadelphia Bar Association's Board of Governors. She is also one of the founders of the Women's Law Project, a coalition of women attorneys dedicated to public policy and education campaigns.

One of only eight women in her starting class at University of Pennsylvania Law School in 1948, a professor predicted this group of female students would "never make it." Norma flourished, however, becoming an editor of the law review and graduating at the top of her class. As law firms were generally unwilling to hire women as attorneys, her law school assisted with placing her as the first female law clerk of a very respected judge on the Pennsylvania Supreme Court. Upon completing the one-year clerkship, she did receive a job offer from a Philadelphia law firm—but as the firm's librarian, not as a lawyer. Instead, she decided to teach legal writing at the University of Pennsylvania Law School. Eventually, she was able to make her way into private practice. After three years of litigating at a firm, she took a leave of absence for nine years (during which time she had her three children and was very active in civic matters); she then came back to the firm in 1967 and was made a partner in 1973. President Jimmy Carter appointed her to the federal bench in 1978.

Lighting the Way

Lifting a piece of paper from her desk, Norma volunteers, "Let me share one of my favorite quotations. This sums up my advice to young women embarking on the journey of a new career. It is from Gaius, an ancient Roman official: 'One who helps the wandering traveler does, as it were, light another's lamp by their own, and it gives no less light because it helped another.'" She then remarks, "When you light the candle in another's lamp with your own, your lamp still shines bright. . . . My lamp has never burned out."

Norma's lamp has, in fact, lit the way for countless travelers, including Phyllis Beck (a Pennsylvania Superior Court judge, the third woman in Pennsylvania to win a state-wide election, and the first to serve on an appellate court). Phyllis recognizes Norma as one of her great supporters. Phyllis, in turn, is a supporter of Norma's. "When I became a judge," Phyllis remembers, "I received a phone call from Norma. She welcomed me to the bench and gave me some advice on getting started. She offered herself as a resource for anything I might need. At professional gatherings, she sought me out. . . . But the wonderful thing about Norma is not that she was nice to me when I was a new judge. It is that I have learned I am not the only new judge to whom she has extended this sort of kindness. So many women who have joined the bench from this area were contacted by Norma. We all think of her as a friend

we can call upon. She is the roots of a tree that is growing and blossoming."
She smiles, "Just call me Norma's number one fan."

Another traveler Norma helped along her way is United States District
Judge Anita Brody. Brody recounts, "After Norma spent fourteen years as the
only woman on this bench, I also was appointed to it. . . . She was elated to
have me join her. . . . She told me she felt like a child who had been waiting
to have a sister—though that did not mean she didn't love her brothers! She
provided invaluable guidance. . . . And I have seen her chambers open to
young women seeking advice from the student level to those seeking public
office. She is dedicated to mentoring."

When asked why she chose to take up a lamp and go out and travel the
hard road years ago when there were few other women on the path, Norma
responds, "There were a number of influences, but I'll share one early one—
a woman I admired but never knew. Florence Allen, a judge of the Ohio
Supreme Court, was this country's first
female federal judge. I wrote an essay
about her in eighth grade. . . . She
inspired me, as hope I have encouraged
others, to pursue a career in the law."

Constructing a Network

Norma explains how she came to value
mentoring. She remembers how, even
though she had "been admitted through
a door" by being appointed to a federal judgeship, she sometimes felt excluded
when she saw what is often called "the old boy network" in action: "I would
be in a meeting with male colleagues, and the name of a man in our professional
community would come up. Invariably, somebody in the group knew him—
from prep school, college, graduate school, sports, military, country clubs, or
time spent practicing at firms. I was amazed repeatedly at how many of their
colleagues my male colleagues knew or knew of. . . . They used this informal
network to move their careers along.

*". . . I recommend not
only networking and
mentoring, but actually
forming a network
of mentors."*

"Women entering the professions lacked this established network—we didn't serve in the military together, we didn't play team sports. We were not made to feel entirely welcome or included by male colleagues. . . . So we tried to reconstruct the dynamic of the old boy network amongst ourselves—in a bit of a contrived way, perhaps. Women had meetings and started organizations with the explicit purpose of career consulting and career enhancement for women. Men didn't do that. They didn't need to. They got to know each other in other ways, and then used those friendships for career advancement. Women had meetings for career advancement, and then became friends and did other things together. . . . Now there's a substantial network out there of women—and men—who are willing and able to help a woman advance after a door has been opened to her."

Mentoring 101

In addition to forming a network of professional friends and acquaintances, Norma recommends cultivating mentor-protége relationships in the workplace. "You learn so much from someone further along in her career who helps you develop your potential," she observes. "It's a nurturing relationship, in which your errors are corrected and your efforts are supported. You learn how to do your job, but you also learn how to fill out the edges of being a professional— how to make decisions that include strategy on the big picture or ethical issues, how to infuse humor into a difficult situation. . . . I also suggest to young women that they find mentors outside of their company or organization to provide career guidance. I even think mentor relationships with people outside your field are helpful. . . . So I guess you could say I recommend not only networking and mentoring, but actually forming a network of mentors."

She describes some of her activities involved in the ongoing business of mentoring: "Some people just need you to listen and provide encouragement. Some ask me a question or two once in a while. Sometimes I sit here counseling someone and I think 'Whom do I know? And whom do my friends know?' so I can provide an introduction needed to help achieve a goal. . . . Some people need information from me. Some want to discuss their plans and solicit advice. . . . It is a joy for me to do all of it. I love spotting new talent and vicariously enjoying the successes of others." She smiles, "I make a lot of new friends in the process.

"If a female attorney told me she wanted to establish a professional presence in the community," Norma elaborates, "I would coach her with these suggestions: Branch out and work for some new people in your firm; develop an area of expertise that people in the firm, clients, or the media will come to you about; teach a seminar in the professional community on recent legal issues; publish an article in a trade journal read by clients, lawyers, and potential clients; participate in a local professional committee, perhaps through the bar association; and get involved in a community endeavor. . . . For instance, I have served as an associate trustee of a university, a trustee of a hospital, as well as a school board president. And I am presently serving as the president of the Jewish Publication Society. . . . The people you meet in these sorts of activities are often leaders in the community, and this is a good way to get to know them."

Norma talks about some ways in which a student might augment school experience through volunteer work and be affected by even a small amount of encouragement from a mentor. For

" . . . Identify what it is you want to accomplish and what you need from others . . . Then think about who could help you—and be able to tell them why you think this.

List the anticipated obstacles you will face in accomplishing your goal, as well as anything that has prevented you from doing so in the past."

example, a college student volunteering to help a lawyer one afternoon a week in a law firm can witness how a lawyer functions, develop various workplace skills, get advice on subjects to study in school, or solicit other career advice. Further, small gestures, such as a mentor adopting language suggested by a student for an article or a speech can have a positive impact on the ego and confidence of the student. Norma comments, "A small thing like that is wonderful, isn't it? Someone sees more in you than you see in yourself and goes out of his or her way to help you. . . . Everyone should take that kind of interest in others."

How to Approach a Mentor

When looking for advice from a mentor, Norma advises that there are a number of things to keep in mind. "First, identify what it is you want to accomplish and what you need from others—training, advice, information, an opportunity, an introduction to someone. Then think about who could help you—and be able to tell them why you think this. List the anticipated obstacles you will face in accomplishing your goal, as well as anything that has prevented you from doing so in the past. . . . Don't define success and achievement strictly in relation to your family or your peers. There are many ways to get to the same place—and there are plenty of great places to go! Think about the paths most suitable for you. . . . Keep in mind you can wander a bit without being lost.

"The helpful role of failure must be recognized." She counsels, "When you experience a failure or a set-back of some kind, assess what went wrong so you can avoid the same problem in the future. . . . Then, when you proceed again, don't proceed in a way designed to protect yourself from other failures. Proceed having learned things about yourself and others or about a situation. . . . Realize that everyone has failures. Not succeeding at something right away—or in the way you want—may cause you to re-examine what is important to you and what your goals will be. Lots of people tell me how a perceived 'failure' helped them to better define their desires and actually assisted them on their way to success. In hindsight, they're happy things did not turn out as they originally hoped and planned. . . . To put today's failure in perspective, write down a few things you've accomplished in the past. Remind yourself of what you had to overcome and how you did it. In the future, today's failure will be a tiny blip on the radar screen."

Norma stresses the importance of being appreciative of those who take the time to help you. "When someone mentors you—and I mean 'mentor' as a person who helps you along your way (he or she doesn't have to be your boss or your teacher . . . it could be a peer)—show your gratitude! Someone has stopped what she was doing to help you with what you're doing. She might have something to gain from it, or she might not. But she extended herself for you just the same. . . . A short note, voice-mail, or e-mail from you saying thanks and letting her know what happened as a result of the effort is appropriate—and it keeps the door open for future assistance. . . .

"A caveat! Be considerate of busy schedules. Don't call in the middle of the workday expecting to discuss an issue that will require an hour. . . . I have found there are plenty of women who feel it is their obligation to mentor other women. . . . So I am always surprised at the disbelief a young woman might express to me when we meet somewhere, talk a bit, and I say 'call me for lunch so we can talk some more.' . . . People sometimes seem surprised that there are those of us who offer help—who look for ways to help others along. Yet, the reason I'm at this job is because I believe in the importance of this country's future generations. . . . I support and defend the Constitution of the United States so our children and their children's children will know the blessings of liberty."

"Not succeeding at something right away—or in the way you want—may cause you to re-examine what is important to you and what your goals will be. Lots of people tell me how a perceived 'failure' helped them to better define their desires and actually assisted them on their way to success."

Improving Communication

Norma suggests others could start to be mentors in the same manner she did: "I used to always tell my coworkers things I wished I'd known earlier. From the positive feedback I received, I discovered I enjoyed helping people."

Norma goes on to share something she has learned in her career that she wishes she had known earlier. "You cannot overestimate the importance of communication skills in the workplace—and in life, for that matter. When you interact with a loved one, an adversary, or a colleague, you must understand the other person before you can hope to influence them. Listen attentively. Paraphrasing in your own words what the other person has said to you is a good tool to make sure you understand. Ask follow-up questions. . . . Communication is not successful because of what you're saying—it is successful based upon what the other person is hearing.

"Communication is not successful because of what you're saying— it is successful based upon what the other person is hearing."

"Improve your reading and writing, your speaking and listening skills. Spend time with words. Read books by good writers. Revise your own writing until it says what you want to say—precisely. Edit your writing until it is polished— until it sparkles! . . . In an information society, words are what we exchange— not our handiwork. Make the way you handle words a craft. Choosing the right words to use can clarify issues and bring consensus."

She also considers being able to speak in front of others an essential career skill. "Project confidence—speak up, loudly and clearly. What you have to say is important enough to be heard. . . . Lawyers standing before me in the courtroom to make an oral argument or an opening statement have known the facts and the case law—but mumble. It is hard to believe they are attempting to convince me or the jury of anything. . . . Some ways to improve speaking skills are by reading aloud, by talking into a tape recorder and reviewing the tape, and by practicing presentations in front of others or in front of a mirror. . . . Practice really does make you better at it. When I served as president of the school board, I was often called upon to give off-the-cuff remarks. Now I never need a rehearsed speech."

A Parting Lesson

Norma comes around from behind her desk and sits on its edge: "One more thing . . . As a woman who started a career in the 1950s, let's just say I suffered countless acts of gender discrimination and harassment. It doesn't matter what they were. There's little to be learned from that. But you can learn from the way I dealt with it. I coped by never assuming that any mistreatment resulted from anything I said or did. . . . Discrimination and anti-feminine prejudice is a defect of the discriminator and a sign of insecurity—not mine, but his. It was a sign that something about me made him uncomfortable. There was something about me he feared. And, as far as I was concerned, he had something to learn."

> *"Discrimination and anti-feminine prejudice is a defect of the discriminator and a sign of insecurity—not mine, but his. . . . There was something about me he feared. And, as far as I was concerned, he had something to learn."*

MARGARET BRENT
AWARD RECIPIENTS

Margaret Brent arrived in America in 1638 with a large land grant. As an unmarried property owner, Brent was able to exercise rights of "court-baron" and "court-leet." Maryland court records show that she appeared in over one hundred cases. There is no evidence of another female lawyer in the United States until the suffrage movement in the late nineteenth century.

In 1991, Senator Hillary Rodham Clinton, while serving as chair of the American Bar Association's Commission on Women in the Profession, established the Margaret Brent Women Lawyers of Achievement Award to recognize women who have achieved excellence, influenced other women to pursue careers, and opened doors previously closed to women.

I met with about twice as many Margaret Brent Award recipients as are featured in *The Counselors*. Time and space constraints prevented further conversations from being pursued or presented. It should be noted that all of the recipients I met, as you might imagine, were uniformly impressive, inspirational, and wonderful.

2001 Honorees
Laurel Bellows, Partner, Bellows & Bellows, Chicago, Illinois

Irma Herrera, Executive Director, Equal Rights Advocates, San Francisco, California

Hon. Gabrielle Kirk McDonald, Special Council on Human Rights, Freeport McMoran Copper & Gold, New York, New York

Hon. Mary Schroeder, Chief United States Circuit Judge, United States Court of Appeals for the Ninth Circuit, Phoenix, Arizona

Marna Tucker, Partner, Feldesman Tucker Leifer Fidell & Bank LLP, Washington, D.C.

2000 Honorees

Sheila L. Birnbaum, Partner, Skadden, Arps, Slate, Meagher & Flom, LLP, New York, New York

Shirley M. Hufstedler, Senior Counsel, Morrison & Foerster, LLP, Los Angeles, California

Hon. Judith S. Kaye, Chief Judge, Court of Appeals of the State of New York; New York, New York

Justice Sandra Day O'Connor, Supreme Court of the United States, Washington, D.C.

Dovey L. Roundtree, General Counsel, National Council of Negro Women, Charlotte, North Carolina

1999 Honorees

Prof. Barbara Allen Babcock, Judge John Crown Professor of Law, Stanford Law School, Stanford, California

Carol E. Dinkins, Partner, Vinson & Elkins, LLP, Houston, Texas

Justice Carol W. Hunstein, Supreme Court of Georgia, Atlanta, Georgia

Pauline A. Schneider, Partner, Hunton & Williams, Washington, D.C.

Hon. Norma L. Shapiro, United States District Court for the Eastern District of Pennsylvania, Philadelphia, Pennsylvania

1998 Honorees

Special Award: **Justice Claire L'Heureux-Dubé,** Supreme Court of Canada, Ottawa, Ontario, Canada

Maureen Kempston Darkes, President, General Motors of Canada, Ltd., Oshawa, Ontario, Canada

Justice Bernette Joshua Johnson, Louisiana Supreme Court; New Orleans, Louisiana

Irma L. Rangel, State Representative, Texas House of Representatives, Austin, Texas

Judith Resnik, Arthur Liman Professor of Law, Yale University Law School, New Haven, Connecticut

Judith A. Winston, former Executive Director, The President's Initiative on Race, Washington, D.C.

1997 Honorees

Special Award: **Roberta Cooper Ramo,** Past President, ABA, Albuquerque, New Mexico

Evelyn Gandy, First woman Lieutenant Governor of Mississippi, Hattiesburg, Mississippi

Jamie S. Gorelick, Vice Chair, Fannie Mae and former Deputy Attorney General of the United States, Washington, D.C.

Antonia Hernandez, President and General Counsel, Mexican American Legal Defense and Educational Fund, Los Angeles, Calfornia

Hon. Joan Dempsey Klein, Presiding Justice, California Court of Appeals, Los Angeles, California

Drucilla Stender Ramey, Executive Director and General Counsel, Bar Association of San Francisco, San Francisco, California

1996 Honorees

Hon. Rosemary Barkett, United States Court of Appeals, Eleventh Circuit, Miami, Florida

Justice Beryl Levine, North Dakota Supreme Court, Palo Alto, California (retired)

Nina Miglionico, Partner, Miglionico & Rumore, Birmingham, Alabama

Lynn Hecht Schafran, Director, National Judicial Education Program/NOW Legal Defense and Education Fund, New York, New York

Patricia Schroeder, United States House of Representatives, Denver, Colorado (retired); President of the Association of American Publishers

1995 Honorees

Special Award: **Hon. Bella Abzug,** former Congresswoman & Cochair, Women's Environmental & Development Organization, New York, New York (deceased)

Justice Shirley S. Abrahamson, Wisconsin Supreme Court, Madison, Wisconsin

Mahala Ashley Dickerson, Partner, Dickerson & Gibbons, Anchorage, Alaska

Prof. Lani Guinier, University of Pennsylvania Law School, Philadelphia, Pennsylvania

Louise B. Raggio, President, Raggio & Raggio, Inc., Dallas, Texas

Ada Shen-Jeffe, Director, Evergreen Legal Services, Seattle, Washington

1994 Honorees

Special Award: Prof. Barbara Jordan, LBJ School of Public Affairs, University of Texas, Austin, Texas (deceased)

Nancy L. Davis, former Executive Director, cofounder of Equal Rights Advocates, San Francisco, California

Jean E. Dubofsky, Attorney, sole practictioner, Boulder, Colorado

Margaret Hilary Marshall, former Vice President & General Counsel, Harvard University, Cambridge, Massachusetts; Chief Justice of the Supreme Court of Massachusetts

Vilma S. Martinez, Partner, Munger, Tolles & Olson, Los Angeles, California

Hon. Patricia McGowan Wald, United States Court of Appeals, D.C. Circuit, Washington, D.C.

1993 Honorees

Special Award: Hon. Janet Reno, former United States Attorney General, Washington, D.C.

Hon. Betty Weinberg Ellerin, Associate Justice, Appellate Division, New York

Justice Ruth Bader Ginsburg, United States Supreme Court, Washington, D.C.

Elaine R. Jones, Director-Counsel, NAACP Legal Defense & Education Fund, New York

Justice Joyce L. Kennard, California Supreme Court, San Francisco, California

Esther R. Rothstein, Partner, McCarthy and Levin, Chicago, Illinois (deceased)

1992 Honorees

Special Award: **Anita F. Hill,** former Professor, University of Oklahoma College of Law, Norman, Oklahoma

Margaret L. Behm, Partner, Dodson, Parker & Behm, Nashville, Tennessee

Hon. Betty B. Fletcher, United States Court of Appeals, Ninth Circuit, Seattle, Washington

Dean and Prof. Herma Hill Kay, University of California Law School (Boalt Hall), Berkeley, California

Rep. Patsy Takemoto Mink, United States House of Representatives, Honolulu, Hawaii

Justice Leah J. Sears, Supreme Court of Georgia, Atlanta, Georgia

1991 Honorees

Hon. Phyllis A. Kravitch, United States Court of Appeals, Eleventh Circuit, Atlanta, Georgia

Andrea Sheridan Ordin, Attorney, private practice, Los Angeles, California

Justice Rosalie Wahl, Minnesota Supreme Court, St. Paul, Minnesota (retired)

Jeanette Rosner Wolman, Attorney, Baltimore, Maryland (deceased)

Marilyn V. Yarbrough, former Dean, University of Tennessee College of Law, Knoxville, Tennessee

RESOURCES

Here is contact information for organizations and causes related to *The Counselors*. I will be donating some portion of any proceeds I receive from the sale of this book to each of the following.

American Bar Association Commission on Women in the Profession

The Commission on Women assists women in law school, law firms, public interest, academia, and the judiciary. The Commission recognizes trailblazing women with its Margaret Brent Award at the ABA annual meeting every summer. It has a newsletter as well as a number of other publications for sale.

ABA Commission on Women in the Profession
750 North Lakeshore Drive
Chicago, IL 60611
Phone: (312) 988-5715
Email: abacwp@abanet.org
www.abanet.org/women

College Summit

College Summit works to increase the college enrollment rates of low-income, academically mid-tier students by helping students show their whole selves to colleges in the application process and by helping schools and businesses to better identify and prepare these students. I have served as a writing coach at College Summit's workshops on college applications.

College Summit
P.O. Box 9966
Washington, DC 20016
Phone: (202) 966-1222; (866) 266-1100
Email: jharrison@collegesummit.org
www.collegesummit.org

Equal Rights Advocates

Equal Rights Advocates uses litigation and advocacy to work for equal rights and economic opportunities for women and girls. Nancy Davis, interviewed for Chapter IX of *The Counselors,* is ERA's co-founder and former executive director.

Equal Rights Advocates
1663 Mission Street, Suite 250
San Francisco, CA 94103
Phone: (415) 621-0672
Advice and Counseling: (800) 839-4ERA
Email: info@equalrights.org
www.equalrights.org

Families for Freedom Scholarship

Former President Bill Clinton and Former Senate Majority Leader Bob Dole are cochairs of a scholarship fund that will provide educational assistance for the children and spouses of those killed or permanently disabled as a result of the terrorist attack on America on September 11, 2001.

Families of Freedom Scholarship Fund
Citizens' Scholarship Foundation of America
1505 Riverview Road
P.O. Box 297
St. Peter, MN 56082
Phone: (877) 862-0136
Email: freedom@csfa.org
www.familiesoffreedom.org

The International Association of Women Judges

The International Association of Women Judges works to promote the rights of women to equal justice around the world. Joan Dempsey Klein (Chapter XI) is a founder of IAWJ.

The International Association of Women Judges
50 F Street NW, Ste. 8312
Washington, DC 20001
Phone: (202) 393-0955
Email: office@iawj-iwjf.org
www.iawj-iwjf.org

Mexican American Legal Defense and Education Fund

The Mexican American Legal Defense and Education Fund works to promote and protect the civil rights of the tens of millions of American Latinos in education, employment, immigration, and voting access. Antonia Hernandez, the subject of Chapter XII, serves as its president and general counsel.

Mexican American Legal Defense and Education Fund
634 S. Spring Street
Los Angeles, CA 90014
Phone: (213) 629-2512
Email: maldefone@aol.com
www.maldef.org

NAACP Legal Defense and Education Fund

The NAACP Legal Defense and Education Fund, Inc. uses the legal system, public education, and policy research to work for the civil rights of African-Americans and other disenfranchised individuals. Elaine Jones (Chapter VIII) is LDF's president and director-counsel.

NAACP Legal Defense and Education Fund Inc.
99 Hudson Street, 16th Floor
New York, NY 10013
Phone: (212) 965-2200
Email: info@naacpldf.org
www.naacpldf.org

The National Association of Women Judges

The National Association of Women Judges has members who are both female and male judges, from all levels of the judiciary. NAWJ strives to improve the administration of justice by working toward fairness, gender equality, and diversity in America's courts. Joan Dempsey Klein, whose story is shared in Chapter XI, is a founder of NAWJ.

The National Association of Women Judges
1112 16th Street NW, Suite 520
Washington, DC 20036
Phone: (202) 393-0222
Email: nawj@nawj.org
www.nawj.org

NOW Legal Defense and Education Fund, including the National Judicial Education Program

NOW (National Organization for Women) Legal Defense and Education
Fund uses the law to work for women's rights—in courts, Congress, state
legislatures, and the media. I work for the National Judicial Education
Program (a project of NOW LDF in cooperation with the National
Association of Women Judges). Lynn Hecht Schafran, Director of the
National Judicial Education Program and the subject of Chapter I
in *The Counselors,* suggests obtaining the *Gender Fairness Strategies
Implementation Resources Directory* from the NJEP to learn more about
what the gender bias implementation committees have done.

NOW Legal Defense and Education Fund and/or
National Judicial Education Project
395 Hudson Street
New York, NY 10014
Phone: (212) 925-6635
Email Helpline: peo@nowldef.org
Email for NJEP: njep@nowldef.org
www.nowldef.org

The Truman Scholars Program

The Truman Scholarship was established by Congress in 1975 as the official memorial to the United States' 33rd President. The Truman Foundation awards scholarships for college students to attend graduate school and to prepare for careers in government and public service. I'm a 1985 Truman Scholar.

Truman Scholarship Foundation
712 Jackson Place, NW
Washington, DC 20006
Phone: (202) 395-4831
Email: office@truman.gov
www.truman.gov

INDEX

ABOUT THE AUTHOR

Elizabeth Vrato is an attorney practicing with the NOW Legal Defense and Education Fund—she is currently working on an initiative to promote gender equality in the legal system. She earned her law degree from New York University School of Law in 1990, where she was an editor on the Moot Court Board. She was valedictorian of her graduating class from La Salle University in 1987 and a 1985 Truman Scholar from Pennsylvania. As a woman in a traditionally male-dominated profession, Elizabeth has sought out mentors and role models and has seen the difference they can make.